Listening With Different Ears
Counseling People Over Sixty

James Warnick

QED Press
Fort Bragg, California

Listening With Different Ears: Counseling People Over Sixty
Copyright © 1995 by James Warnick

First Edition

10 9 8 7 6 5 4 3 2 1

QED Press
155 Cypress Street
Fort Bragg, CA 95437
(707) 964-9520

Cataloging in Publications Data

Warnick, James , 1937–
    Listening with different ears : counseling people over sixty / by James Warnick.
        p.   cm.
    Includes appendices, aids, bibliographical references and index.
    ISBN 0-936609-31-1 (case)   ISBN 0-936609-28-1 (pbk.)
    1. Aged—Counseling of—United States.   2. Aged—United States—Psychology.   3. Social work with the aged—United States
4. Gerontology—United States.   I. Title.
HQ1064.U5W373 1994
362.6'6'0973—dc20   93-48690
                                                                             CIP

QED Press would like to thank publicist Belvie Rooks for her guidance and expertise. We would also like to thank John Fremont, Sal Glynn, and Chuck Dunbar for their editorial assistance and Neva Beach for her continuing support.

Preface

When I began working as a counselor of *third-age people*,[*] I had good credentials—a master's degree in Gerontology and a master's degree in Human Development Counseling. Although most of my counseling experience had been with seventeen-to-twenty-one-year-old boys, I believed I knew what to expect from my sixty-plus clients. Yet rarely did a day pass without my encountering situations and patterns not mentioned in the counseling or gerontology books. To meet these challenges, I developed some attitudes and approaches to help me better serve my clientele. What follows are six patterns or situations that were ignored or merited only a footnote in my formal education.

1. I was amazed to find strong linkage between my clients' concerns and their early years.

---

[*] The term third age may be new to some readers. Rather than using conventional terms such as the elderly, senior citizens, the old, or older people, I favor third age. The conventional terms are sometimes the vehicles of ageism, discrimination against people sixty-plus, which is rampant in our society. Understanding and grasping the importance of these patterns I believe is what separates the exceptional from the average counselor.

When I began counseling third-age people, I considered myself a cognitive behaviorist and tended to emphasize today's problems rather than those of ten or fifty years ago. Most books emphasize the effectiveness of a cognitive behaviorist approach with third-age people. While I still use this approach, I also found an unexpected degree of dysfunctional living in my clients: half were divorced in an era when divorce was taboo; others had great difficulty dealing with people. With a little probing, I found that about 40 percent of my clients had experienced a difficult childhood, and had suffered emotional, physical, or sexual abuse, or all three. Moreover, almost all who had difficult early years also had difficult and stressful lives. When they had reached their third age, it seemed that they had used up so much of their emotional reserve they could not deal with the challenges ahead of them. I developed the formula:

Difficult Childhood + Dysfunctional Adult Life = Vulnerable Third Age

When I encountered an individual who'd had a difficult childhood, I subtly made certain we talked about that childhood. The purpose was not to alleviate all the problems the abuse in childhood had caused, but to help my client put these negative experiences in perspective. I wanted him or her to understand how the past may have impacted the present.

2. I began to view anxiety, depression, and alcoholism as mere symptoms of unhappiness.

Although I initially began working with individuals in a conventional counseling manner, I soon focused more on the causes rather than the symptoms. And causes varied tremendously: difficulty dealing with health problems and with relationship problems; frustration with governmental programs; economic problems; and, in some instances, concerns with situations that had taken place fifty years ago. Regardless of the cause, I urged clients to discuss difficult periods, events, or concerns that made them susceptible to what I viewed as mild mental illness. After the person had time to talk, think, and deal with a concern, the symptoms of anxiety or depression often disappeared. Whereas an emotionally strong person could deal with their concerns, or adjust and adapt, most of my clients seemed more vulnerable. I had to help them understand that they had done as much as could be expected in dealing with a concern. The symptoms of anxiety or depression often appeared when they would consciously or subconsciously berate themselves for not dealing with the concern. Once they understood that they had made an honest effort, they seemed to recover.

3. About 20 percent of the time I served as problem solver rather than counselor.

In some situations I found I could help a client more by solving a problem and dealing with the cause rather than treating the symptoms. As a result, I found myself mediating in family disputes, serving as a personal envoy in disagreements with bureaucracies, helping people find jobs, fix plumbing, and do a variety of other tasks. In time I realized that what I was really doing was convincing clients that they had at least some control over their lives. I saw that symptoms of mental illness often appeared after an individual started feeling helpless, feeling that his or her life was out of control. A problem-solving approach enabled me to accomplish much more in a brief period of time.

4. I was amazed at the immense power my clients gave to me.

After winning their trust, I worked at empowering my clients to make their own decisions, whenever the potential for taking control was present. Because they found themselves in a vulnerable situation, many questioned their ability to make decisions and wanted my input. They knew that they could offer any idea or thought to me without being judged. (Family members are usually all too eager to judge the actions or thinking of other family members.) I also found that the best way to discourage too much reliance on my help was to offer my clients various options and encourage them to make their own decisions.

5. I did lots of informal "zinger" counseling.

Don't look for an explanation of "zinger" therapy in the index of any textbook. Because many of my clients were somewhat lonely, they looked forward to my visits with great anticipation; someone overhearing our sessions would have thought them friendly conversations rather than therapy. Sandwiched between friendly comments were what I call therapeutic zingers—observations that bolstered people. For example:

- "I knew that wouldn't be difficult for you."
- "You handled that situation very effectively."
- "That's the way she's always treated you. Expect it to happen and feel thankful when she doesn't put you down."

One important point a session is sufficient for a counselor to achieve success, and a point can be made just as effectively with a zinger as with an hour of intense focus on a concern.

6. Counseling techniques are relatively unimportant.

When studying for my master's degree in counseling, I paid great attention to counseling techniques—the saying of the right word and the asking of the right question at just the right time. These counseling techniques are important, but in working with third-age people, the element of trust is far more important. If the client believes the counselor has his or her best interests at heart, the counseling relationship will be successful. I am not at all certain that a person can "learn" to establish trust. I once had a classroom disagreement with a professor who maintained that anyone could learn to become a counselor. I argued that some people are not psychologically suited to counseling. I have since worked with several counselors who had read all the books, knew all the techniques, yet lacked the capacity to establish a strong rapport with clients and as a result, were only moderately effective.

Looking back, I believe that textbook authors have failed because they attempt to put every client into a little box. If a person has a certain symptom, the textbook-trained counselor is instructed to deal with that person in a specific way. The weakness of this approach is that textbooks can only establish so many boxes, yet each client is an individual with a unique past and a unique set of concerns. Although you can take a conventional approach with some clients, other clients require a unique approach. Regardless of approach, however, every client deserves the considered intercession of a caring counselor.

Table of Contents

Acknowledgments

I OFTEN TELL MY CLIENTS that we all have a history, that what we are at the moment has been a lifetime in the making. This book also has a history. Many people, both knowingly and unknowingly, participated in its creation.

A plethora of teachers at Sangamon State University, where I earned my graduate degrees in Gerontology and Human Development Counseling, provided the foundation. My cohorts at the Decatur Mental Health Center, where I worked during the writing of this book, provided consolation and the freedom for me to "do it my way." Of course I must thank Cynthia Frank and John Fremont of QED Press, who believed in the potential of this book. Chuck Dunbar's suggestions during the editing process greatly improved the book. Finally, I must thank my wife, Glea, director of Social Services at Decatur Memorial Hospital, who during our thirty-minute drives to and from work served as my unofficial consultant.

Although all these people contributed greatly to this book, my clients deserve the most credit. (I have changed all names and in specific situations made other alterations to protect their privacy.) When my clients were hurting, they provided the motivation for me to do my best. When I deviated from the counseling norm, my clients very subtly informed me about success or failure. When on occasion I wondered about the progress of a client, that person would make a remark that provided fresh motivation.

The day before I wrote this acknowledgment, for example, a ninety-two-year-old client, who calls on me every couple of months, smiled after we had discussed her concerns. "Mr. Warnick, I want to do something for you. You've done so much for me. What can I do for you?"

"Rose," I replied, "you can call me Jim. I've been trying to get you to call me by my first name for more than a year now."

"Okay, I will. See you next time, Mr. Warnick."

Section One

INTRODUCING THE THIRD AGE

Chapter 1

Why Counsel the Third Age?

S ome therapists believe third-age clients cannot be counseled effectively. They maintain that people old enough to receive Social Security checks are too rigid and inflexible to respond to counseling, and that their problems result more from the aging process than from situational difficulties. They question expending energy on clients whose life expectancy is so short. They believe that working with this age group is not only difficult but senseless.

These skeptical professionals rarely acquire their pessimism from personal experience—most of them have had little experience with this population—but from having heard second- or third-hand reports of the difficulty involved in accomplishing goals with third-age clients. Their only experience may have consisted of working with a family that included a third-age parent.

On a more personal level, many counselors find that working with third-age clients provides them little status compared to marriage and family counseling. Surely, working with a vibrant thirty-five-year-old whose fee is paid by company insurance is more glamorous than working with a seventy-five-year-old living on a $600-a-month Social Security check. The counseling profession has almost ignored third-age people.

Government-supported agencies have ignored the counseling needs of this population almost as much as the counseling profession.

A woman once called me about her father, who lived in an eastern city with a population of 100,000. The eighty-year-old man had lost his wife four months earlier and gone into a deep depression, mentioning suicide. The city did have a crisis intervention center, but not one agency or counselor who dealt specifically with third-age people. The only possibility for help was an agency offering adult outpatient counseling, and it had a five-week waiting period.

Counselors and governmental agencies have generally ignored the counseling needs of third-age people, and placing the responsibility for this situation on mental health professionals is unfair. Research indicates that although 15 to 20 percent of the third-age population might benefit from counseling, only 2 percent seek help, the result not only of a lack of interest by the mental health community but also because of certain attitudes and myths within the third-age population. These beliefs perpetuate an "I-can-do-it-myself," rather than a "Maybe-I-need-help" attitude. Many third-agers view counseling as a sign of weakness, a stigma to avoid, and a service too expensive to afford.

This negative attitude will change in time. New generations will be more sophisticated and better educated, and other groups will be more accepting of help from social service organizations. Women, in my experience are more likely than men to seek assistance, and those at the lower and upper end of the economic scale more readily receive help. (Those with more money are frequently more sophisticated in recognizing that counseling can help, while those with little income are subject to governmental subvention.) The most resistant group to counseling seems to be white, middle class men.

Although research indicates that fewer than half of the general population seeking counseling has found it beneficial, more than 50 percent of the third-age clients my agency has worked with have benefited. This is not because counselors in my agency are experts but because third-age people, contrary to belief, are far more receptive to counseling than other age populations. When I reviewed my last hundred clients, I found that thirty-six had made considerable progress, forty-nine had made some progress, and fifteen had made no progress.

Even the most effective counselor can never solve all the client's problems. Sometimes these concerns are so severe that they defy resolution; most of the time the degree of progress depends upon the individual. What characterized the 15 percent of my clients who made no progress was the inability to allow change, or the refusal to allow me to help them.

One of the tasks of the counselor is to instill in the client the motivation to accept help; however, some clients simply prefer to go on hurting. Generally speaking, the third-age client who refuses to cooperate with a counselor now might also have failed to cooperate with a counselor twenty, thirty, or forty years previously.

The counselor who chooses to work primarily, or even part-time, with third-age people will discover that counseling them is simultaneously the same as working with other age populations, as well as different. It is the same in that although individuals have their own unique qualities, they often react to problems in remarkably similar ways. Depressed people tend to react in basically the same way regardless of age. This sameness of reaction has allowed mental health professionals to conceive the *Diagnostic and Statistical Manual of Mental Disorders*, which describes how people react to specific problems.

Three Characteristics of Third-Age Counseling

Although unique pressures exist at every stage of life, those that burden third-age people are different and more intense than those that impinge at other stages of life. Pressures that affect people in their twenties, revolve around lifestyle decisions. Pressures affecting third-agers arise from threats to the tranquillity in which they seek to live the last third of their lives. Situations sometimes develop that make tranquil third-age living difficult or impossible.

Counselors usually begin working with third-age clients when they are in a crisis so severe that they are impelled to ask for help for the first time. Sometimes when clients or family members ask for help, the distress has reached such an intolerable level, that clients (who may never have been in counseling before) will share their innermost thoughts. A client who had lost her adult son to an unexpected heart attack suffered immense anguish in the nine months following his death, commenting that for the first time she felt she had lost control of her life. After the second session, she looked at me with astonishment. "I'm amazed. I've told you more about myself than I've ever told anyone else." And she felt immense relief from talking about her anguish.

Despite unique pressures, despite severe crises, third-age people are more capable of change than people at other stages of life. After all, they have lived longer, had diverse experiences, and gone through more changes than people in earlier stages of life. Imagine the adjustment de-manded after the loss of a spouse to whom the partner had been married for twenty to sixty years. The survivor will grieve, flounder, and drop to the lowest depths then right himself or herself and begin once again to enjoy life. The person who can successfully undergo such a transition is not the inflexible individual portrayed in most books that describe the third age.

Challenges await the counselor in each third-age client. Although the thought of seeing a counselor may seem to most clients an admission of weakness, their lives may be in such turmoil that they are willing to deal with it in the hope of finding relief.

Periodically I back away from my clients to look for patterns. Effective counselors always look for patterns of thinking, reactions, and behavior, and I have noticed three general situations in many clients' lives. Al-though sometimes situational causes exist in isolation, often the client will have at least two and sometimes all three situational causes working in concert to create a concern.

1. In Transition

Counselors of third-age people for the most part work with people *in transition;* i.e., in circumstances that force people to move from one life-style to another. The person who loses a spouse moves from a lifestyle as part of a couple, albeit each part with different roles and obligations, to the lifestyle of a single person. This transition becomes more difficult if the surviving spouse has never lived as a single adult. Not only must the third-ager adjust to the loss of a significant person, but also to living a dif-ferent lifestyle.

Clients with health problems provide another example. When a basi-cally healthy person encounters health problems, he or she must make a transition from a healthy lifestyle to an unhealthy or restricted lifestyle.

One of my clients experienced pulmonary problems and went from liv-ing a normal lifestyle to living hooked up to an oxygen tank in her home and pulling a portable tank when she left home. Not only did she have to deal with the restrictions of the oxygen tank, but she also suffered from the severe anxiety problems that sometimes accompany pulmonary diffi-culties.

A recent retiree provides a third example of a person in transition. Where some individuals delight in not having to work at a scheduled job, others experience major difficulty adjusting to this situation. A husband leaving the stimulation of the workplace may find that getting up every morning with no concrete demands is disastrously dissatisfying. Another retiree may experience problems with spending more time with a spouse as a couple, and marital problems result. A single person may become unbearably lonely without the friendships of the workplace.

Obviously one may make these difficult transitions without experiencing any adjustment problems, while another may have difficulty adjusting to a new situation. Individuals who have difficulty making transitions sometimes seek the assistance of a counselor.

2. In Trauma

Closely related to *in transition* is *in trauma*, which occurs when the third-age person experiences such a traumatic experience that he or she has great difficulty making the transition or dealing with a problematic situation. Where *in transition* occurs over a period of weeks or months or years, *in trauma* results from a single traumatic event. Generally speaking, stress becomes trauma when it:

- occurs without warning.
- is overwhelming.
- is overwhelming to such a degree that it cannot be tolerated.

When a person has an in trauma experience the powerful event may totally upset his or her life. The person can think of nothing else and relives the event repeatedly. Often the person feels vulnerable and helpless because of what happened. Such an experience can result from the unexpected death of a spouse or a close friend. A child's death promotes serious trauma. Other example of trauma are muggings, robbery, or serious health problems.

Some problems with trauma do not fit into any defined category. I once had a client who called the crisis center with this problem: her eighty-two-year-old brother had for a year been asking her to have sex with him, and for that year her life had been a disaster. The older brother, a charming, retired minister who was nine years older than she, had served as the titular head of the family. Once a month he drove my client to a veteran's hospital a hundred miles away where another brother was a resident. For the first three years of these monthly trips, the journeys were delightful for both of them. However, at the beginning of the fourth year the brother suggested that my client sleep with him.

This request was so unexpected, so unthinkable, and so overwhelming that my client had much the same response as if she had been raped: her health deteriorated and she became extremely nervous and unsettled. Finally her family physician, who had treated her for thirty years, recognized that something was wrong and suggested she contact our program. Working together, we managed to reduce the trauma to an unpleasant memory. (She protected her brother, and I never had an opportunity to work with him.)

Sometimes an *in trauma* experience leads to an *in transition* crisis. A couple was referred to me for marital counseling. Five years earlier, the wife's health problems had resulted in her early retirement. Her husband assumed the role of caregiver, and the two had been fighting nonstop for five years. The wife had always been the dominant force and the primary economic provider. When she could no longer fulfill these roles, the marriage crumbled under the pressure. She became more domineering and tyrannical, and he responded by becoming combative. But because the couple was motivated to change, they regained a measure of their previous "tranquillity" through counseling. This situation provides an example of how a trauma (the wife's illness) resulted in a transitional crisis (the husband's difficulty in adapting to a new role).

3. Dysfunctional Background

When I first began working with third-age clients, I immediately noticed the overwhelming presence of dysfunctional elements in the backgrounds of some of my clients. While taking family histories, I noted the presence of alcoholic parents, personal problems with alcoholism earlier in life, divorces in an era when divorce was considered unacceptable, instances of emotional, physical, and sexual abuse, and extensive signs of family discord. I found numerous situations in which clients had not spoken to parents, siblings, or even adult children for years. Due to the underlying strain of serious family discord, it was as if any disagreement provided justification for ending a relationship.

I found that often the problems involved daughters-in-laws or sons-in-law. When I first visited Charlotte, a client who was referred to me because of chronic pain and numerous trips to the hospital emergency room, I found her to be a pleasant, sixty-eight-year-old woman living in an old, but clean, small house. When I asked about her family history, I found that she had been divorced twice. Her second husband was in jail for molesting two young girls. She had refused to get a job and had lived a marginal life for years on the alimony of her first husband. She had not seen one of her sons for several years, although he lived only ten miles away.

"It's my daughter-in-law," Charlotte said, in describing her estrangement from her son. "We got along fine for twenty-five years. Then one day she called and said she didn't want to see me anymore and that she didn't want my son to see me either. That was five years ago. I've seen my son once since that time, at a shopping center." This situation typifies what I have found in 90 percent of the situations in which a parent and adult child are estranged: the adult child is totally dominated by a spouse who caused the estrangement.

Although I have never done a thorough study of this, I estimate that about half my clients were normal people who encountered situations that were simply too difficult for them to deal with. The other half had difficult early years and lived somewhat dysfunctional lives. When I visited Gertie, a client who lived in a subsidized apartment and whose husband had died two years earlier, I expected abnormal grief to be at least part of the problem. But Gertie dispelled that perception. "No, it didn't bother me none when he died," she said. "We were married for fifty-one years but only lived together for five years. He was an alkie. He worked all the time—just drank like a fish when he was off work."

In exploring the situation further, I discovered that of her two children, one son was estranged because the woman he was living with would not allow him to visit Gertie. And she had a lukewarm relationship with her daughter. However, Gertie seemed to have a close relationship with her three granddaughters, two of whom had married and divorced alcoholics or drug abusers. The third was a young widow—her husband had been a heavy drug user who committed suicide.

Many of my clients are people who had somewhat dysfunctional early years but who had lived relatively stable lives until encountering the pressures of the third age.

Although these three situations do not totally explain the reason why some people have difficulties when they reach the third age, they do provide an explanation for many problems. Pressures of the third age attack everyone. Perhaps eight of ten people will cope well with these pressures, but the remaining two will have difficulty; however, this book is not about the majority of the population that copes well with the pressures of the third age but about the minority that has difficulty coping.

Counseling third-age people involves aiding individuals who have difficulty with transitions, who have experienced traumas, or who have suffered abuse or problems earlier in life. If working with this age population is both the same but different from working with other age groups, how does the counselor work effectively? What techniques does the counselor use? What works? What doesn't work?

Before answering these questions, let's take a look at the problems third-age people typically encounter.

Chapter 2

Pressures of the Third Age

We are not all equal under the law. Although we may be equal when we enter a voting booth, once we emerge from that booth equality ends. As we move through life, the inequalities multiply. Some people are born with great innate intelligence potential; others must live with a much smaller intelligence potential. Some are born into a stable family environment and possess balanced, secure personalities; others are born into dysfunctional family environments that play havoc with their lives. Fate smiles on some, frowns on others.

Because of the inequalities of life, how a person enters the third age varies tremendously. Some enter as secure individuals who can deal with the stresses of this stage of life. Others are insecure and wilt at the first hint of challenge. But security or insecurity begins at birth rather than on the day the first Social Security check is received. With each passing day the inequalities dealt by genes, environment, and innate coping mechanisms multiply.

Life is a process and the process includes a series of crises. These crises vary in intensity from created situations such as "I must have a new bicycle," or "I must have that job," to life altering crises such as "Why did my father have to die so young?" or "I don't deserve to get this cancer." These crises do not decrease when the first Social Security check arrives; often the crises become more severe. How these crises are dealt with depends in part on what has happened during the previous stages of life.

Although several authors have written effectively about the stages of life and how people react and live through these stages, I prefer the approach of Gail Sheehy in *Passages* and *Pathfinder*. As people pass through different stages of life, they change; relationships change; how society views and treats them changes. As a result, they acquire a different perspective towards life and towards themselves. Sometimes this perspective is positive and sometimes it is negative. Gail Sheehy describes these stages this way:

In the "Pulling-Up-Roots" stage (eighteen to twenty-two), people leave the security of the nest and tentatively begin to feel their way in the world. Those who grew up in favorable environments usually get jobs or go to college. Those who grew up in unfavorable environments may turn to street crimes or just sit and watch the world go by. Regardless of which road is taken, or which road is open, people begin establishing their individuality. Sometimes personal changes can be made with great bravado. Other times, situations over which there is no control force people to accept change.

In the "Trying Twenties" stage (twenty-three to twenty-seven), Gail Sheehy observes that people begin to establish their identities. If they went to college, their identity is linked to their profession. If they did not go to college, their identity is often liked to progress up the job ladder. In addition , "Trying Twenties" people begin seeking intimacy from others. This is the stage of life when most marry and begin (or at least consider) a family.

In the "Catch-30" stage (twenty-eight to thirty-three), people begin to question their lives. They wonder if they have made correct decisions in relationships, marriages, careers, and family. This questioning has a major impact on the lives of many people. Wives who may have stayed home to raise children cannot wait to return to the work force. Others change careers, spouses, or lifestyles.

In the "Deadline Decade" Stage (thirty-five to forty-five), people recognize that they are mortal. In this stage they use the calculator: "If I am forty, I have perhaps forty years of life left." Because the countdown has begun, some live with inner turmoil that may be fueled by hormonal changes. Once again, relationships, marriages, and careers may be questioned.

In the "Comeback Decade Stage" (forty-six to fifty-five), people change perspectives. They wonder what is really important, and questioning and changes sometimes continue. By the time hormonal changes have ended, people have also adjusted to aging parents and to children leaving the nest. Interestingly enough, where men in their fifties become less interested in careers and more interested in enjoying themselves, women often become more assertive, managerial, and interested in careers.

In the "Freestyle Fifties" stage, many people live what may be the happiest period of their lives. Reinforcing earlier shifts in thinking, men get a better perspective on life and stop being overly concerned with careers. Women in this stage begin accepting their physical image and stop belittling themselves for every perceived physical imperfection. As women battle and hopefully conquer societally-induced problems of low self esteem, they start thinking of personal needs rather than the needs of others. Some women become interested in careers and in compensating for lost time. On the whole, men and women grow closer and take more pride in the companionship of their love partners.

In the "Selective Sixties" stage, people may ignore aspects of their lives that formerly troubled them. And as Gail Sheehy notes, an important task of the sixties is to decide: "How long do I want to live?" If they decide in favor of longevity, they often quit smoking, drinking to excess, lose excessive weight, and become part of the crowd that exercises early in the morning. During the selective sixties, people "select" what is important.

In the "Thoughtful Seventies" stage, the happiest people are those who continue living independently and continue making plans for their lives. When people stop making plans and begin living day to day, this sometimes means they have given up and live only because their bodies continue to function. Most people in this stage of life become pensive and thoughtful as they ponder the meaning of life.

In the "Proud to be Eighties" stage, many people live a fragile life with boundaries set by a deteriorating body. However, this stage includes people who are proud of their achievements, and of having actively lived for so long. They are determined to live considerably longer. I remember being in a class listening to an eighty-plus woman who spoke, looked, and acted twenty years younger. When asked her age, the woman proudly responded, "I'm eighty-two and a half." What I found interesting was that although it was a three-hour class, the eighty-two-year-old woman stood at the side of the room rather than sat on a chair. In other words, she neither thought nor acted like most eighty-two-year-old women.

The stages of life consist of twists and turns that many, perhaps even most people experience. In many ways, the stages of life resemble Elizabeth Kubler-Ross' five stages of death (anger and isolation, denial, depression, bargaining, and acceptance). Most people go through the five stages in succession, although some people will skip a stage or two, go through the stages in different order, or become stuck in one stage and never get beyond it. People do not go through stages of life in exactly the same way. Some people enter their third age with the perspective of someone in the "Trying Twenties." Someone else will be "Proud to be Eighties" when in their forties.

Generally, however, people who enter their third age with strength and stability have taken each twist and turn at an approximately appropriate time.

Psychological Transitions

Traveling through the stages of life, is like going through school. Although most people begin and complete the first grade, the inequalities of heredity and environment make subsequent grades an easy learning experience for some and a major obstacle for others.

So, too, with the aging process: a person who has difficulty transitioning from one stage of life to another often has problems with later stages. On the other hand, if one adjusts well on the journey through life, reaching the third age will not pose major difficulties.

When people reach third age, they must make several psychological adjustments, and to a great degree how they fare in third age depends upon how effectively they adjust and adapt. The following perspective derives from the work of Erik Erickson, Robert Peck, and others.

During the growing-up years, females emphasize personal appearance and males emphasize physical prowess, perspectives that place major burdens on both men and women. Because of societal demands, women may allow their physical appearance to determine their personal worth. As people mature, they begin valuing wisdom more than appearance or physical prowess. Studies reveal that women do not begin feeling comfortable with themselves, with their physical appearance, until they reach their early fifties. In this respect, women mature positively. To the contrary, when men begin losing their physical prowess, they sometimes view themselves extremely negatively.

I grew up on a farm, and I remember a man whose physical strength had deteriorated to where he could no longer bale hay. "I'm just not much good any more," he remarked. His physical strength was far more important than the wisdom he had gained over a lifetime of farming.

As people mature, they value companionship more than sexuality in relationships. During early adulthood, the sexual aspect of relationships predominates thinking. Sometimes people marry because of this preoccupation. Only later do some of these couples discover that they have nothing in common, that they may not even like one another. Such immature relationships almost always fail.

Also, when people mature, they must be flexible in order to deal with change. When they leave the workplace, for example, they redefine their roles as humans. Retirement is especially difficult for men whose identity depends on their work role. Likewise, the traditional woman whose major role has been caring for a husband and children may experience great difficulty when the children leave home and the husband dies. A flexible person can call upon a lifetime of experiences to find answers to new issues, a person who has become rigid often has difficulty adjusting to life.

Finally, people must accept the reality of death. How well the reality of death is accepted differs with each stage of life. It is much easier to accept the concept of death after having lived a long life than it is to face premature death. In this respect, it is much easier to accept death if the body has become frailer than if one is in good health. Accepting the reality of death does not mean dwelling on the inevitable; it means glorying in each new day. People who do not accept the reality of death often dwell on it instead of living what is left of their life.

Third age people are not inflexible and incapable of change. Look at the amount of change that is built into the third age—retirement, death of significant others, and the reality of one's own death. The third age requires tremendous change, and those who deal with these changes positively weather the pressures of the third age with comparative ease.

Pressures of the Third Age

Each stage of life contains its unique pressures, and most people experience these pressures at least in degree. How someone responds to the unique pressures of the third age provides an indication of individual differences. One person may suffer tremendously from these pressures and allow them to dominate his or her life, where another may barely notice their existence. What a person is in life becomes exaggerated in the frail years; a secure person becomes stronger; an insecure person becomes more insecure.

It would take an encyclopedia to describe the pressures and combinations of pressures a third-age person might feel, but here are the top ten:

1. Lifestyle Changes

Most people enter the third age with an informal master plan. They are going to travel, fish, sit in the sun, read books, or, if married, they plan to live together until very old and frail and then die together. If they have grandchildren, they will thoroughly enjoy their grandchildren, and so on. Although sometimes these plans work out, often they do not. Sometimes the planned activities prove boring; sometimes one spouse dies ahead of the other and decades are spent alone in a couple-oriented society. Even though an idyllic life in the third age is planned, sometimes the unexpected occurs, and sometimes there is difficulty adjusting and adapting to a changed lifestyle.

2. Losses

Although suffering the loss of a spouse or other significant person is the most obvious third-age loss, there are other potentially debilitating losses as well. When a person loses mobility, ceases driving, or avoids using public transportation, that person's life changes drastically. Where some people become prisoners in a house or apartment, others remain mobile by adjusting to what happens. Personality, resolve, and degree of family support affect a person's capacity to deal with immobility and isolation. An introverted loner will adjust better to loss of mobility and isolation than an extroverted individual who needs people.

3. Relationships

Relationships sometimes change drastically when people enter their third age. Sometimes an older man married to a younger woman wants to travel or move to another part of the country while his wife still remains tied to a job. A couple can retire together and then find that a relationship that was relatively strong deteriorates because of too much togetherness. Other people find themselves caught between competing generations—caring for a eighty-eight-year-old parent on one side while dealing with adult children or grandchildren on the other. Relationships change when parents and the children or grandchildren change roles. Sometimes this change is positive; other times it can be highly stressful.

4. Health Problems

The effect of deteriorating health as the body ages, cannot be overemphasized. The payback for a lifetime of neglect or abuse might mean dealing with the illness itself, the side effects of medicine, occasional inept medical professionals, guilt from pressures placed on others, an outside world that often doesn't care, and sometimes with all these situations at once. Not only do health problems result from negative health habits of earlier years, but these problems also may result from genetic deficiencies and fate. Maintaining one's health requires considerable effort, but the reward is worth the effort: walk through a nursing home filled with people whose health has deteriorated, and observe the residents' restrictive lifestyle.

5. Fears

As people move into their frail years, some experience additional pressures because of fears. They might feel less in control, less capable of handling problems and situations that occur. Perhaps even because of chemical changes in the brain, people might begin fearing the unknown. Fear of losing their sight or hearing, of developing Alzheimer's Disease or other dementia, of living alone in their homes or apartments, or of being the target of thugs and criminals, are just a few of the fears that afflict third-age people. Although sometimes these fears are justified, often they result from earlier insecurities.

6. Being Treated as Old

An additional pressure that varies with intensity from individual to individual is being treated as an "old person." Some people are openly disdainful of third-age people, especially those in their frail years. Common examples are everywhere: lack of patience with slowness of movement in the supermarket; insensitive remarks; families assuming control of the lives of aged parents or grandparents; and a general assumption that if the legs don't work well there must also be something wrong with the mind. In a letter to a columnist a reader wrote of the discrimination of ageism: "Some mornings I take my daily walk wearing an old jacket and a pair of jeans, carrying a writing pad and pencil in hand to jot down thoughts and observations. When so preoccupied, I often slow down to write a few lines. Someone looking out the window might mutter to himself or herself, 'I wonder what that old duffer is up to.' When I dress for church or to handle business errands, I look more like the successful professional man and am graded as vital and effective—not as an 'elderly' person."

7. Frustration

A client who lived in a high-rise, a woman in her early sixties, had been in an auto accident that had resulted in a stroke that left her partially paralyzed on one side. The paralysis was severe enough to restrict her to a wheelchair and a walker, and she had only partial use of her right hand. "I just sit here and stew all day long," she told me. "Things that used to be so easy for me are now so difficult." Because of her disability, she felt more frustration at her new lifestyle than most third-age people, but other people who have lost the vigor of youth, live a more restricted lifestyle, and believe they have lost some control over their lives, feel great frustration and view the world as a hostile place.

8. Grief

Grief can cause pressure that, if not dealt with normally and effectively, can devastate, and sometimes even end a person's life. I once worked with a woman whose husband had died two years earlier, yet she was living her life as if his death had occurred two weeks ago. She was in reality "stuck" in stage one of the grief process. Feelings of intense grief may not be limited to the loss of a spouse or other significant person. Health problems, or any of the situations mentioned in this chapter, can evoke uncontrollable sadness.

9. Accumulation of Life Problems and Life Attitudes

I believe that the insecurities or securities that a person acquires during life become magnified upon entering the frail years. I have observed that calm, serene, "have-it-all-together" people deal well with the pressures of the third age, while rigid, inflexible, nervous people become even more brittle and suffer increased difficulties with these same pressures. Worries increase, frustrations increase, and when this happens, health deteriorates.

10. Economic Problems

Some people who reach their frail years, are financially secure, others live with a small nest egg, while still others live on the edge. A 1990 *USA*

TODAY poll revealed that prior to retirement, seventy-five per cent of people place great emphasis on having adequate funds. After living in retirement for several years, only twenty-five per cent thought money important. What I find amazing is that some of my clients live comfortably and securely on $600 a month, whereas others have difficulty living on ten times that amount.

Although economic problems pose a major source of pressure for some people in their third age, the amount of money available has little connection with their happiness.

If one overriding problem dominates the third age and seems woven through other pressures and problems that mark this stage of life, it is the very real fear of loss of control over one's life. Sometimes people are forced to adapt to lifestyles that they dislike. The loss of loved ones, changes in relationships, anything might result in the assumption of control by children, or worse, indifferent strangers. The problems that have plagued them throughout their lives become magnified. There may not be enough money. But most frightening of all is what tomorrow will bring.

Obviously some people live for today, adjust and adapt, and pay little attention to these pressures. In fact, the majority of people do not find themselves in the scenarios described above. But third-age people who cannot cope require assistance in dealing with these pressures. They need the help of a counselor to survive.

Chapter 3

Counseling Mechanics

If a roomful of counselors was asked to define counseling, a roomful of different answers would result. Counselors have different approaches. Some are assertive and directive, others prefer a passive and more indirect approach. Some rarely suggest medication for clients, others regularly suggest medication. My approach is a mix of four elements: supportive therapy—in which I undertake any appropriate action that will help my client to regain normality; cognitive therapy—in which I correct the skewed thinking that accompanies anxiety, depression, and the like; medication—as a last resort or in situations where it is obviously appropriate; and adjustment therapy in which I adopt a direct or indirect approach, providing counseling or problem-solving that suits the needs or personality of the client. When dealing with third-age people, there is no "typical" client. All are different.

Despite the variety of counseling approaches, and realizing that counselors probably choose approaches that mesh with their own personalities, most counselors would agree upon the following three basic tenets of counseling:

1. The Potential for Change

Rarely does a third-age client visit a counselor and announce, "I want to make major changes in myself." When the counselor sees a client, it is usually because that client is in crisis from encountering an untenable situation. I have seen many third-age clients who have lived a lifetime without even considering seeking counseling, but who are now extremely agitated or depressed. These individuals are hurting so much they seek the help of a stranger. Most counselors understand the limits of help. For myself, I want to help clients through their crises and provide them with some insight into themselves and how they deal with society. As counselors, we can only offer limited relief.

In the case examples that follow, the clients possess varying amounts of what might be called "change potential." Clients seeking help for depression caused by the inability to deal with problems, can sometimes be helped to make major changes. The counselor may help uplift a depressed person and enable a client to understand the pressures that have created the depression. Such a situation provides relatively large change potential because the counselor can work with the client on altering specific goals that will in time deal with the specific situation. However, I have also worked with clients with very little change potential.

Consider the client who has had multiple strokes and is lying in a nursing home with little chance of recovery. With this person, the goal might be to develop the motivation to go to physical therapy on Thursday.

2. Accepting the Client

When you start working with a client, it may be difficult to approve of, like, or sanction your client's behavior or thinking, but you must resist any temptation to become critical or judgmental. People who believe they are being judged simply back away and refuse to share their beliefs and feelings. Carl Rogers insists that counselors extend *unconditional positive regard* to their clients. No matter what your client says or does, nothing should shake his or her faith in your concern and support.

What separates effective counselors from ineffective ones is the ability to withhold judgment and to convey unconditional positive regard to the client. The effective counselor accepts the client for who he or she is and works within that framework.

A cantankerous man had major pulmonary problems and could not live alone without assistance, but he was belligerent, critical and racist. Bill consistently criticized and harassed people sent to help him, especially black helpers. As an intermediary I did not try to change values anchored in concrete, but I did try to help Bill understand the reality of his situation. After winning the confidence of this sixty-six-year-old man, I said, "Bill, your opinions are your own. You can believe anything you want. But if you want these services you're going to have to change how you treat people." We talked about the trade-off involved: services in exchange for treating the service providers differently. This approach worked, although periodically I would receive a call from the agency that had referred him that Bill was being too cantankerous. I would once again visit Bill and subtly remind him of the trade-off necessary to continue services.

3. Working with the Client

One of the unhappiest individuals I have ever met repeatedly directed invectives at her mother, who had died forty years earlier. Despite Sylvia's anger and unhappiness, she quit after the fourth session. Not only were her problems so severe that she could have benefited from intensive therapy, but she also wanted me to do all the work. She was unwilling to work with me in a collaborative effort to reduce her anguish, preferring to spend the sessions spewing anger at her dead mother, rather than assume some responsibility for what had created her discomfort.

The counselor is not a dictator of beliefs, giver of advice, changer of attitudes, or worker of miracles. Counselor and client must work together as a team in helping the client deal with concerns that are upsetting. The counselor nudges the client toward goals as rapidly as the client will allow. The client who succeeds must be receptive to these gentle nudges, for an uncooperative client will rarely achieve progress. The client in crisis is usually so unhappy that he or she will cooperate without question. However, when I began seeing Sylvia, she was not in a state of crisis but in a state of unhappiness that had existed for forty years. To deal with her forty years of unhappiness would have required a great effort on her part, a degree of personal introspection Sylvia refused to make. She did not want to assume responsibility for her feelings.

All counselors would agree that limited change is possible, that counselors should accept the client as he or she is, and that the client should work together as a team with the counselor. Every counselor would like to lead the client a little further, but for the most part counseling, and especially counseling third-age people, moves forward in tiny steps rather than in great leaps and moves only as far as the client will allow.

Theorists separate client counseling into five stages: building the relationship, assessment, setting goals, intervention, and termination. Of the five stages, building the relationship is probably the most important. A counseling relationship is built upon trust, without which the most skilled clinician will not succeed.

1. Building the Relationship

Of the five stages the most important probably is building the relationship. No matter how effective you are at assessing situations, setting goals, and selecting intervention strategies, counseling will not be effective unless a close relationship is developed with the client. If you have poor rapport, your client will probably cease coming or find excuses to avoid counseling sessions after the third or fourth session.

Counseling rapport resembles love on a different level. Counselor and client develop a certain chemistry between them; when this chemistry develops, a link is established. The client believes that he or she can say anything, share innermost thoughts, and ask any questions or ask for any observations. The counselor accepts these feelings, thoughts and observations without judgment or disparagement. A degree of success having already been guaranteed, you can experiment with various goal-setting or intervention strategies. You will not always be the perfect counselor. Counseling rapport happens over time and translates into the establishment of complete trust between counselor and client.

When I look at myself as a counselor of third-age people, I see someone who is good in technique and the mechanics of counseling, but particularly effective in building rapport. The ability to establish strong rapport, will enable you to overcome a lack of expertise in other areas. In working with third-age clients, rapport becomes far more important than mechanics.

Establishing strong rapport is especially important with third-age people because they often enter the counseling relationship suspicious and skeptical about the worth of the counseling process. If rapport does not dispel your clients' suspicions and skepticism, all is lost, but establishing rapport with a third-age client in the midst of a personal crisis is not difficult. The more severe the crisis, the easier it is to build a positive counseling relationship, for the potential client is reaching out and searching for relief.

Generally speaking, the three qualities that create a strong rapport between counselor and client are empathy, sincerity, and positive regard. Empathy permits the client to accept that you have moved into his or her world and understand the concerns that necessitated seeking your help.

Sincerity convinces the client that you really want to understand and help deal with these concerns. Sincerity also reveals that the counselor is not a phony, but shares the clients' concerns. Positive regard demonstrates that the counselor respects and accepts the client no matter what he or she says.

These three qualities may develop individually, but all are linked. To assist you in establishing these qualities:

- *Reflect and paraphrase what the client is saying:* "What you are telling me is that... Is that correct?"
- *Reflect emotions:* "You're feeling very angry about..." "I see that...made you very sad."
- *Reward the client for small steps forward:* "I can see a major improvement in..."
- *Demonstrate verbal and nonverbal attentiveness* to the client by speaking in a pleasant voice, showing interest, relaxing with an open, leaning forward posture, and maintaining an open, welcoming approach.
- *Build rapport* by creating an atmosphere of trust, providing a vehicle with which the client can exchange innermost thoughts, and by motivating the client to deal with concerns.

2. Assessing the Client's Concerns

Assessment of the client's concerns begins with the first telephone call and continues in the relationship building stage. It involves collecting information and making a diagnosis. The counselor defines the client's concern and searches for the means to help the client deal with it. These means have been described classically in counseling theory as needs, stressors, misinterpretations, and patterns.

A *need* might be defined as something that is missing in a client's life, and this missing component keeps the client from achieving a desired fulfillment. With third-age clients, the need might be translated as a desire to regain what once existed. The third-age client frequently enters the counseling process because of anxiety or depression. These symptoms often result from underlying situations—the death of a spouse, health problems, or other losses. The counselor may help the client regain normalcy by dealing with the problem of anxiety or depression and simultaneously with the underlying problems of abnormal grief due to the loss.

A *stressor* is a situation or unpleasant event that is pressuring the client or interfering with his or her life. Sometimes the stress is closely related to need, but other times it may be a specific event. I worked with a woman whose husband was in a nursing home because his Alzheimer's disease had reached a point where she could no longer care for him, but the husband's children, who were the wife's stepchildren, pressured her to remove the husband from the nursing home because of the cost. The adult children believed nursing home care was consuming their inheritance. The children thus placed considerable pressure on their stepmother.

Misinterpretation is a faulty way of thinking that affects or limits a person's life. Some third-age people do this all the time. Sometimes a person will believe that he or she cannot live without a spouse or job. A client may believe that having attained a certain age, the time has come to sit in the house and do nothing. Or the client may feel irrational guilt for any number of reasons. Regardless of the stressor or misinterpretation, people may develop skewed thinking or a skewed mindset.

A *pattern* is a specific behavior exhibited by the client in specific situations. A dependent wife who loses a spouse may believe that she cannot balance a checkbook, drive a car, or assume any of the responsibilities formerly performed by the departed spouse. In such instances, the counselor should help the client become more assertive. A person suffering from depression may assume that everything will always go wrong—a pattern of learned helplessness.

More than likely these situations do not appear in isolation, but in clusters or in combinations. One of my clients had never worked outside the home and was almost totally dependent on her husband. When he died, she grieved normally for her departed spouse and felt her life could never be the same (the need). Because she had always been dependent on her husband, it was stressful for her to live independently (the stressor). Because she had never functioned independently, she believed she was incapable of living without her husband (the misinterpretation). Because of all this, she simply sat in her home and cried (the pattern).

Assessing a client includes two major components: information gathering and problem definition. I often survey the family history during the second session, when it is appropriate. By listening to the client's concerns in session number one and taking a family history in the second session, you can accomplish several things. By not challenging the client in session one, you build rapport; In session two, in addition to collecting factual information while doing the family history, you can ask a few subtle questions to determine whether the client has had a stable or a dysfunctional childhood and life. By the time the family history is revealed, your client has become accustomed to talking about personal matters, thus facilitating the counseling process.

Many assessment tests are available to the counselor: family history outlines, problem definition outlines, and brief tests for levels of stress, anger, anxiety, depression, and cognition. Selective use of these aids depends on your judgment and intuition. Each assessment is unique. With some clients I have been able to use several tests early in the counseling relationship, but I first made sure I'd established rapport with them. Insensitive use of information gathering aids can interfere with building rapport. On the whole, I avoid using tests and becoming too mechanical in my approach. Only when I encounter a truly appropriate situation will I use such tests.

3. Setting Goals

Helping clients deal with their concerns involves setting goals, which might coincide with setting short-term objectives that eventually lead to the final goal. Sometimes the client needs to become more confident and assertive. An unassertive person has probably spent a lifetime in passivity, so helping the client become more assertive requires time and effort.

There are two kinds of goals: process goals and outcome goals. Process goals help the client deal with concerns and are not achieved in one gigantic step. Clients climb these stairs one step at a time, realizing one short-term objective after another. Outcome goals are the final change that, in working with the client, a counselor seeks to achieve. In helping your client achieve an outcome goal of dealing with grief, for example, you can establish a series of process goals, such as getting out of the house, re-establishing friendships, meeting new people and so forth.

Goals allow you and your client to gauge progress. They act as motivators, helping clients feel good about themselves and possibly acquire new ways of thinking and behaving. Most important, goals provide a valuable tool in working with third-age clients, enabling the counselor to take a concrete approach and to discuss specific thinking that leads to specific actions requiring specific changes in thinking and behavior. Rather than merely urging the client to become more assertive or take control of his or her life, the counselor proposes concrete actions the client may take.

4. Intervention

In the first three stages of counseling—establishing rapport, assessing needs, and setting goals—the counselor basically creates support for the intervention stage. In this stage, a counselor often tries to help the client in three ways:

A) The counselor helps the client deal with the concern that initially prompted the need for assistance. The concern may be depression or anxiety that is more a symptom of an underlying problem, in which case the counselor must deal with both the symptoms and the underlying problem.

B) The counselor helps to restore a client's damaged self-esteem. An inability to deal with concerns is often accompanied by a loss of self-esteem, which is made up of self-concept and self-worth. In turn, self-concept, or belief in who we are, is composed of reflected appraisals (how we think others view us); social comparisons (how we compare ourselves to others); self attribution (conclusions made about ourselves); and psychological centrality (how we value our qualities). Self-worth is the value that we attach to ourselves. Because of role changes, perceived pressures, and ageism, many third-agers suffer societal attacks on their self-esteem, resulting in diminished self-concept and self-worth. Through intervention strategies, the counselor helps rebuild the damage to a client's self-esteem as well as dealing with symptoms and concerns.

C) The counselor helps the client acquire some insight to help deal with new concerns that may arise. Third age concerns come not individually but in clusters, with one situation creating several concerns. Counseling that helps the client deal with one concern should also help with other concerns. As a counselor, you cannot choose clients to fit your counseling strategy; you must choose a counseling strategy to fit the client. Effective strategies are supportive and cognitive. Used in concert, these therapeutic tools work best with third-age clients because supportive therapy involves *feelings* and cognitive therapy involves *concrete means of dealing with these feelings*. Let's examine these tools more closely.

Supportive Therapy

Uniquely tailored to the needs of third-age people, supportive therapy includes major elements of Carl Rogers' client-centered therapy, but goes further because the counselor is more directive, more actively involved than Carl Rogers envisioned. In supportive therapy, the counselor helps the client move from a state of maladjustment to a state of adjustment by helping the client express feelings, discriminate between feelings, and alter feelings. In talking about feelings and concerns, the client is motivated to examine the troubling aspects of these concerns. In this sorting out of feelings and concerns, the counselor often immediately recognizes how the client should deal with a concern, but rather than telling the client what to do, the counselor nudges the client into making these discoveries.

One of my clients spent the bulk of her time worrying about whether her daughter, who treated her shabbily, really loved her. I could have said, "Martha, what you need to do to deal with your depression is build a life without your daughter." Rather than be this directive, I let Martha make the discovery herself. After the fifth or sixth session, she looked at me and sighed: "I guess I have to think of a life without worrying about what Karen does." From then on, she made immense improvement. The key to "talking therapy," as some people like to call it, is for the client to realize what is the real and often not apparent concern. The counselor can facilitate the dawning of new awareness, but the client must do the work of understanding and integrating this new perspective into his or her life.

Two-thirds of my clients have maladjusted beliefs about normality. They believe that something is wrong with them because they are having difficulties, most commonly in dealing with grief. After a couple of sessions of encouraging a client to talk about how they miss a dead spouse, I like to point out that it is normal to be still grieving after six months or a year. This usually provides tremendous relief to a client who fears the worst. After one such observation, a client told me, "I feel so much better. I thought I was losing my mind." By helping the client understand that it's okay to feel sad, the counselor contributes to correcting maladjusted thinking about what is "normal."

Supportive therapy goes beyond talking therapy by expanding the concept of support. I frequently visit clients at home, and this helps them relax considerably—especially during the initial sessions. I also keep the sessions as informal as possible. I may spend 80 percent of the time discussing what has happened to the client since our last session. Sometimes I promote an informal life review by inquiring about the past or the growing-up years. I may be the only person the client has spoken with recently, unleashing a great amount of information that the client wishes to release. I seek an opening to make a crucial point, or to reaffirm a client's crucial observation. A client's voluntary observation is worth numerous questions.

Some of my clients look to me for other kinds of support. I have fixed air conditioners, transported clients, adjusted glasses, and performed a hundred tasks that required only a few minutes of my time but helped to build rapport and trust. Most of these tasks, while easy for me to do, presented major obstacles for the client who does not drive or see very well. Obviously I do not take this approach too far, and I watch out for manipulators, but this is part of support, and the approach enhances the effectiveness of talking therapy.

Cognitive Therapy

Cognitive therapy maintains that people manifesting symptoms of depression or anxiety suffer from distorted perceptions of themselves and from problems based on personal relationships that perpetuate distorted perceptions. Three general principles emerge:

A) People's moods are created by their thoughts.

When a person feels bad, and believes that life is hopeless, a mood is created that reflects this thinking. The mood of the moment results from the thought of the moment. Thoughts and beliefs about one's life create emotion—a person who engages in negative thinking creates a negative mood. A client who suffered from pulmonary problems that required oxygen almost all day remained in her house, hooked up to her large tank. Although she had a portable oxygen tank, she rarely ventured outside to resume her life. I have also seen people in almost every situation, pulling their oxygen, living their lives. These individuals consider their oxygen tanks a minor inconvenience, but my house-bound client doubted her capacity to cope outside her house and because of this negative thinking, she thought herself into depression and isolation.

B) Depressed people's thoughts are dominated by a negative mindset.

Take two people who have both lost a spouse. Both are grieving, both believe their world has been destroyed, but one person believes that after a normal period of grieving life will again be good; the other believes that life will never again be good. The person with the negative mindset may never recover from depression and may go through life continually viewing every experience from a negative perspective, while the person who views life with a positive mindset slowly recovers from depression and lives a vital, enjoyable life.

C) Depressed people with a negative mindset grossly distort every happening, twisting positive happenings into negative happenings, always expecting the worst.

Receiving a promotion doesn't make any difference; jobs aren't important anymore. Receiving a large inheritance becomes twisted to, "It's just money. I can't enjoy an inheritance without… " When a person has a negative mindset that leads to gross distortions, no matter what happens becomes negative.

Negative Problems + Negative Moods = Negative mindset

Negative mindset + Gross Distortions = Unhappiness

Practitioners of cognitive therapy maintain that a counselor can deal with depression, anxiety, and other situations by changing the client's pattern of thinking. In cognitive therapy (described in detail in the Appendix), the counselor works at replacing negative thoughts, a negative mindset, and gross distortions with reality. Once the counselor has replaced negativity with a positive view of reality, the client discards the distortions of a situation and deals with the symptoms of depression or anxiety that have dominated his or her life.

Cognitive Therapy and Third-Age Clients

When used in conjunction with supportive therapy, cognitive therapy is especially effective in working with third-age people. Basically a short-term therapy, cognitive therapy allows the counselor to get in, deal with the distortions, and get out. Typically, the time required in treating depression is six to twelve weeks rather than the extended period required by other therapies. In some situations, the counselor uses medication with cognitive therapy.

Many of the problems faced by third-age people don't result from childhood emotional abuse but from situations encountered in the third age itself: ageism, grief, loss, and other major problems that create a warped perception of one's self. Cognitive therapy works to deal with these warped perceptions created by environmental or lifestyle situations.

Cognitive therapy is successful with third-age people because it is concrete. It is a "do something" therapy. Although supportive therapy is important and fulfills a valuable function in the therapeutic process, most third-age clients understand how a person's mind can warp the world and will work at dealing with these distortions.

Utilizing brevity of treatment, responding to problems resulting from situations, and emphasizing concreteness of treatment afford the practitioner of cognitive therapy several advantages when working with third-age people. Because it is practical and based on common sense, most third-age people understand and welcome it.

Regardless of approach, you will try to accomplish three objectives:

A) You want to help your client gain an understanding of personal concerns.

Through attentive listening, cognitive homework, observations, and gentle nudges, you will help your client understand his or her concerns. Although counselors lack the time to conduct long-term analysis, they may help clients understand how the past affects today. You will find that almost every client has had numerous difficulties in the past that make it difficult to deal with the present.

B) You want to help your client realize that he or she owns the problems, concerns, and issues.

Your client must recognize and accept personal responsibility for his or her life. Some clients immediately blame other people for every difficulty. Although there is no doubt that other people sometimes create major problems, your client must come to accept that, he or she owns the problem and must deal with it. The origin of the problem is immaterial. When your client acknowledges ownership of an issue, a concern, or a problem, he or she is accepting responsibility for what happened earlier in life and accepting responsibility for actions or behaviors in the future.

C) You want to help your client first consider and then choose ways of thinking and behaving.

A client will experience success only if effective new ways to deal with the concerns that have created difficulties are freely chosen. While you may nudge your client into understanding feasible options, the client must make the final decision to choose new ways of thinking and new patterns of behavior.

5. Termination

Terminating the counseling relationship is a relatively simple transition for some clients and difficult for others. Most clients understand that when goals have been reached the sessions will soon end, but clients who have become dependent on the counselor may want to hang on, for the counselor may be the only person in whom the client can confide.

Termination should begin with the first session. State at the beginning that the program is limited to fourteen sessions or four months. When you are three or four sessions away from termination, begin subtly talking about the successes that have so far been achieved and mention that termination is not far away. When I start referring to termination, I also clarify that should the client have difficulty in the future, he or she can always come in for a few sessions or perhaps even another fourteen sessions.

Termination should fit the specific client. Clients who have dealt effectively with their concerns are usually ready to quit; others might prefer that the sessions continue because you have become their friend; still others will continue to have concerns that require additional assistance. One client appears in the doorway every six months or so and asks for help in dealing with a crisis. As with other stages of counseling, remain flexible and adjust to the needs of the client.

Chapter 4

Considerations When Working with Third-Age People

In some ways working with third-age clients is the same as working with other age populations, and in some ways it's quite different. Here are ten considerations that are unique to or magnified in third-age clientele. When assessing third-age clients, keep these aspects in mind.

1. Remain flexible.

A local health clinic referred Clair, a woman about to succumb to anxiety. Her husband Sam had been disabled by a stroke and would spend the rest of his life in a nursing home. Because they had little money, Medicaid would pay his nursing home bill, but Clair worried about how she would live. Sam received $516 a month from Social Security; which went to the nursing home; she received $323 to live on, and she did not know if she could survive on this amount. I could adopt a conventional supportive/cognitive therapy role to help her deal with her anxiety, or I could help her deal with her financial problem. In Illinois, the Spousal Impoverishment Act stipulates that when a spouse is placed in a nursing home on Medicaid, the spouse remaining in the home must have enough to live on. (A spouse living at home can keep the family home plus up to about $67,000 in savings. Most states also have an income limitation test, which varies from about $800 to $1,700. A few states have no income limitation.) In Clair's case, she was allowed to keep both Social Security checks. Once I explained how the law worked, Clair's anxiety decreased drastically.

The counselor's role differs a bit with each client. Sometimes you function as a conventional counselor, using the same techniques with a seventy-five year old client that you would use with someone thirty-five. Sometimes you become a case manager, monitoring the client and arranging for services. Sometimes you become an active listener, simply allowing the client to talk out frustration. Sometimes you adopt a take-charge role and become quite directive. And sometimes you become an advocate and attempt to correct a mistake as I did with Clair. Your role may consist of a combination of the above roles, with your role changing as the client moves from one stage to another.

2. Listen carefully.

Once a month I speak to a local group: retirees from a factory, club members, a support group for people sixty-plus, senior center attendees, etc. One day I received a call from a woman who had attended a meeting at which I had spoken six months earlier. "I have problems cleaning my house," she said. "I procrastinate. The newspapers pile up. The kitchen gets dirty. The house becomes such a mess that I don't want to invite people over." Listening, I got the impression something unspoken was of deeper concern. In time, the real story surfaced. Lily was a highly educated college teacher who was having trouble adjusting to retirement. She was lonely, had few friends, and felt helpless, frustrated, and agitated.

Third agers in such distress that they seek counseling are truly hurting. Yet it also may be their first contact with someone in the mental health field. Sometimes they feel guilty for having to ask for help. Often they don't know how to play the game as do long-time recipients of mental health services. Regardless of the cause, they camouflage what is really happening. The counselor must be prepared to listen and to subtly probe to find the cause for the distress.

3. Watch for organic problems.

Jane called me one day about her mother, Thelma, an eighty-two-year-old woman who lived in fear of a former neighbor. Thelma had lived for several decades in a small house with her husband. Although the neighborhood had begun to change, they had no problems until her husband died.

A family moved in across the street, lived a quiet life, bothered no one, and got along well with neighbors, but Thelma was convinced that the

neighbor was watching her. After this unsubstantiated suspicion continued for a year, Jane helped her mother move into a high-rise apartment
building for seniors. However, the paranoia continued. Thelma believed
her former neighbor was sitting in a car outside the apartment building
watching her window.

Mention of late onset delusions or paranoia by your client or by someone making a referral should alert you to the possibility of an organic
problem—often Alzheimer's disease. The initial symptoms of Alzheimer's disease are sometimes paranoia and delusions, rather than memory
problems. Depression may accompany these symptoms, as people understand that something in their mind isn't working right. Usually the key to
treating this condition is medication. Medication may not eliminate the
symptoms, but it can reduce the impact. I managed to get medication for
my client, but she refused to take it, and continued to live in fear of every
car parked across the street.

4. Help with real-life problems.

Sometimes problem-solving is far more effective than counseling. I had
just returned from a home visit one day when Frank brought his mother,
Myra, into the mental health center where I worked. Myra was crying. Frank
was apologetic. The situation became clear within five minutes. Myra had
two feuding adult children. Frank was dutiful, hard working, and dependable. His sister was a free spirit who lived to the beat of a different drummer.
Although both loved their mother, they disliked one another intensely. This
conflict had intensified to the point where the two had recently scuffled in a
public place. Their conflict had so devastated Myra that she was simultaneously agitated and depressed, unable to sleep. In this situation, I became a
mediator, moving back and forth between each individual, helping them realize that much of their problem was miscommunication. When they realized that their differences were not as substantive as they believed and that
they were hurting their mother, they managed to be civil to one another.
When Myra saw that her children were capable of contact without destroying one another, her symptoms disappeared, and she resumed her full life.

Sometimes the causes of mental illness are beyond the help of a counselor. When a situation is correctable and you can become an advocate, a
problem-solving approach may be effective. Knowing that someone is attempting to resolve a difficult situation may in itself reduce the symptoms
of depression or anxiety.

5. Ask about childhood experiences.

Melissa's daughter called to tell me that her mother was again having difficulties. "My mother has never been a happy person," she said. And the daughter was right. I had worked periodically with Melissa for more than a year. When I first met her, Melissa was in the midst of a major depression. Together we helped her return to normality. However, a series of family ups and downs had again sent her plummeting into depression. This time it was so severe that she had to enter the psychiatric ward of a local hospital to recover. Anyone knowing Melissa's childhood would not be surprised to hear that she had never been a happy person. Her father had simply left one day. Her mother died when she was twelve, and she had gone to live with an aunt who confiscated her meager inheritance and paid a man $50 to marry Melissa. Married at fifteen to an abusive husband, she was married four times in all and had five children, all of whom had their share of difficulties. At times, Melissa was the rock of Gibraltar to her children, helping them through their travails; at other times she was responsible for added concerns. In a way, it was amazing that Melissa was as stable as she was.

Although I consider myself a deal-with-today counselor, I always inquire about my client's past. Do this subtly. Ask about the mother and the father and how the siblings got along. Ask what was the happiest time in your client's life; then ask what were some of the most difficult times. When a person with a difficult childhood begins discussing that trying period, he or she often provides considerable information. A person who had a difficult childhood often has difficulty dealing with the challenges of the third age.

6. Use zinger therapy with some clients.

I began working with Barbara, a sixty-two-year-old widow, after she had spent a week in a psychiatric ward. Even when she was on the ward, Barbara was always smiling, always the gracious, charming host. In time, I learned that Barbara's mother had abused Barbara emotionally throughout her childhood. This emotional abuse continued during Barbara's adult life, and the abuse made Barbara a tenuous woman. When I visited her each month, we always had coffee and conversation. I allowed Barbara to set the tone for the conversation. Intensive, focused counseling seemed to make her uncomfortable, as if she felt disloyal by discussing her troubled relationship with her mother. At some point during our session, however, Barbara would describe an incident involving her mother. This provided an opening for a zinger. I would describe how this incident was part of the pattern and how it probably affected Barbara. "That's right! That's right!" she would reply with a smile. Then we would return to discussing other things. Interestingly enough, a moment of enlightenment seemed enough to sustain Barbara for a month.

With zinger therapy, the counselor follows the lead of the client in conversation. Then at an appropriate opportunity, the counselor makes a pertinent point that the client will hopefully integrate into his or her perspective.

I use a very informal counseling approach. Even in times of great stress, I like to find a reason to laugh and to joke, and without fail the client will find humor in the situation or remark. Some clients want a conventional, focus-on-the-concern session, but others prefer a more informal approach. With clients who prefer a more informal session, I try zinger therapy but follow the lead of the client.

7. Help with important decisions.

Hazel's daughter, Lynn, lived several states away, and was pressuring Hazel to sell the house and move into an apartment building near her. Hazel thought Lynn treated her with disrespect. Hazel told me of the time she visited her daughter, and Lynn, after picking her up at the airport, drove back to the house and immediately went into another room and began reading a book. It seemed obvious that all Hazel would find, after selling her house and moving near Lynn, would be unhappiness. After clarifying the situation, I gave Hazel several options for dealing with her daughter's attitude. Hazel listened, pondered the options for a couple of months, and then asked me to write Lynn a letter. In a rough draft, I described Hazel's point of view. (Hazel approved my draft, making only a couple of minor suggestions.) But Hazel didn't mail it immediately. In fact, she let the letter lie on her desk for nine months. Then, when her daughter came out to visit her, Hazel gave her the letter. With the letter and a bit of mediating, Hazel and her daughter achieved a new closeness.

The key to an effective counseling relationship is trust. When you have your client's trust, you also have considerable power over that client. Do not abuse that trust or power by attempting to make decisions for your client. Simply clarify the available options and allow the client to make the decision—even if your client does not make a "correct" decision.

8. Reinforce your client's strengths.

Everyone liked Anne. A smiling, personable woman in her early seventies, Anne volunteered at a local hospital and enjoyed an active social life. Beneath her smiling face, however, was a woman who had faced difficult times; years before she had ended a marriage to a very cold man. Because the marriage ended after a business failure, Anne received no alimony. She had, in effect, traded a good economic life for a life of poverty. She also had two adult children with their own unending difficulties as well as numerous medical problems. Anne lived her life on the edge. Sometimes because of all the pressures, she forgot her many strengths. Periodically, I had to remind her that she was productive, supported herself, provided support for her children, and had lots of friends. She did everything possible to keep herself stable, and for the most part she was successful.

We all have strengths and limitations, but when we lose self-esteem, we often acquire a distorted perspective and lost sight of our strengths. The counselor has an obligation to remind clients of their strengths and to help build on them.

9. Adjust to your client.

I received a call one day from a woman who said that her father, Ralph, was sitting across the table from her and threatening suicide. After calming Ralph, I began exploring the circumstances that had led him to consider this action. Ralph was illiterate and hearing impaired, a combination that resulted in his not understanding many things about the world. He had been threatening suicide because of hospital bills. After a stay in the hospital, he began receiving bills that had not been paid by Medicare. Billing by hospitals is so complicated, even literate people often cannot figure out what they owe. This situation was especially difficult for Ralph because of his disabilities. I talked with his creditors and arranged for him to pay $60 a month for thirty-six months—just as if he were buying a car. When he understood that he could deal with the situation, he felt great relief. With tears in his eyes, he reached over and patted my shoulder. I still stop in to visit with Ralph on occasion. We have yelling conversations: I speak loudly so he can understand what I say; he speaks loudly because that is way he talks. The last time I saw him, he smiled and pointed to his face: he had grown a beard just like mine.

Adjusting to your client may mean allowing him or her to control the pace at which the sessions progress, or having shorter sessions if the client tires easier. It may mean drinking coffee from dirty cups, sitting on couches that are roach infested, or listening to the same stories over and over. Do what needs to be done to help your client.

10. Close sessions on a positive note.

I saw Sophie about once a month for a year. She'd had a difficult time as wife and mother, and now a daughter-in-law was creating major problems for her. Because this was not a situation in which I could intervene, I had to convince Sophie that she could adjust to the situation: her daughter-in-law Marie had always been a troublemaker, probably always would be a troublemaker, and Sophie had to accept this rather than hope for miraculous change. But sometimes Marie would get to Sophie. When this happened, we would again review the situation, discuss the daughter-in-law's behavior, and discuss ways Sophie might handle the situation. In the process, we discovered a ritual for ending our sessions. Sophie had once told me that her favorite psychiatrist had called her a "tough old broad." From that session on, when I left Sophie, I said, "Remember now—you're a tough old broad." Each time, she laughed loudly at the comment. Being called a tough old broad was a major compliment.

When I close a session, I try to end with an observation of what the client might be working on next week. In making this observation, I note how far the client has moved from the beginning of our sessions. In this way I emphasize the client's strength.

In working with third-age clients look for ways in which your clients' age may affect them. Affecting variables may range from skepticism to a feeling of helplessness to having lost control of life. Not only will you have to deal with your clients' anxiety or depression, you will also have to decide what approach to use and how to provide the motivation that will enable them to again assume control over their lives.

Section Two

MAJOR PROBLEMS OF THE THIRD AGE

Chapter 5

Anxiety, Depression, and Abnormal Grief

Although no two clients have exactly the same problem or react exactly the same way in similar situations, it is possible to put problems into general categories. Variations also occur when clients develop concerns from several categories. One category of illness may be little more than a symptom for another category. Anxiety and depression, are almost always symptoms of other concerns. You will almost always deal with at least two categories of problems in which one is a symptom and the other an underlying problem.

I once attended a workshop on medication and depression led by a psychiatrist from a midwestern university. Since the workshop was aimed primarily at helping family physicians prescribe medication for patients suffering from depression, I expected the workshop to have a medication orientation; however, I did not expect the psychiatrist to say that "medication is the best way to deal with depression. Counseling rarely works."

I found his view of the benefits of medication versus counseling extremely narrow! It's true that some individuals have tendencies toward depression that result primarily from chemical imbalances in the brain. With this kind of client, medication is almost always required. However, chronically depressed clients are very much in the minority. In most clients, depression is little more than a symptom for other problems. You can help such a client by working with both the depression and the underlying problem. Sometimes an antidepressant helps, but it is rarely the focus of the healing process.

Anxiety

Depression is sometimes described as concern for the past and anxiety as concern for the future. While this is generally descriptive, anxiety is much more complicated. Research indicates that the anxiety of almost every third-age person increases with aging. It appears to increase mildly in some individuals and by great leaps in others. Scientists suspect that this increase in anxiety probably results from a change in brain chemistry.

There are two kinds of anxiety: chronic anxiety and situational anxiety. Because of low self esteem, inherent tendencies, unhappy events or a combination of these situations, some individuals experience chronic anxiety all their lives. More people suffer from situational anxiety, or fear of the future. Sometimes this fear results from uncomfortable situations; at other times it reflects the unknown. As people in their third age move past the active years and into the frail years, they fear new lifestyles and losing control of their lives. Often you will be able to relate situational anxiety to a specific environmental event—losing a spouse, losing mobility, or the like. Regardless of the source, anxiety can wreak havoc in a person's life.

Symptoms of Anxiety

Classic symptoms of anxiety include a pounding heart, clammy palms, a gnawing apprehension, or a vague, undefined sense of danger. The world may seem hazy or foggy. Sometimes an anxious person may feel confused, have difficulty reasoning, may be unable to concentrate, and may view the world through a skewed perspective in which failure and negative things are expected to happen.

As the body reacts to anxiety, blood pressure may increase or decrease. Some people faint. Breathing may become rapid or shallow. Insomnia, tremors, pacing, and a feeling of weakness often accompany anxiety. Loss of appetite, nausea, and vomiting are frequent symptoms. Faces often become flushed or pale.

Counselors often have difficulty distinguishing between anxiety and depression, for there are overlapping symptoms. In their fine book, *Anxiety Disorders and Phobias*, authors Beck, Emery, and Greenberg provide a list of six underlying differences between anxiety and depression:

1. A depressed person views the world negatively; an anxious person becomes more selective and may feel anxiety only when dealing with specific situations.

2. A depressed person sees the future as being without significance because he or she has given up; an anxious person sees some positive elements in the future because he or she has not given up.

3. A depressed person believes he or she is defective and worthless; an anxious person does not regard his or her specific life or mistakes as irrevocable.

4. A depressed person believes in absolutes, and believes life is worthless; an anxious person has a more tentative view of life and the world.

5. A depressed person regrets the damage that depression has done to his or her life; an anxious person anticipates the damage that anxiety might do to life or to his or her relationships.

6. A depressed person believes that nothing positive will ever happen to him or her; an anxious person believes that only specific events will go badly.

Causes of Anxiety

Specific life events or threats can create anxiety, and it is not uncommon for someone who has lost a spouse or must cope with an illness to experience extreme anxiety. Other times anxiety may accompany an illness. Anemia, asthma, low blood pressure, heart disease, and pulmonary problems have created symptoms of anxiety. Heredity is also a factor: studies have found that 55 percent of individuals suffering from chronic anxiety have relatives who suffer from high anxiety, but only 2 percent of the general population have close relatives with higher than normal anxiety.

Many third-age people suffer increased levels of anxiety due to chemical changes in the brain.

Anxiety may appear without a discernible cause. It sometimes is rooted in the mind. Other times it is rooted in the body. Often several of the above situations may act in concert. A person may have a hidden genetic tendency toward anxiety which may surface as a result of stress from a life-event, a medication, or an illness. Reaction to a specific food may trigger a reaction. Often the counselor can discern the cause of anxiety in the client, but the cause can also remain hidden, in which case you must deal with the symptoms without knowing the underlying cause.

Dealing with Anxiety

Helping third-age people who suffer from anxiety can prove perplexing. No single approach seems to work all the time. In dealing with depression, most counselors use a specific approach much of the time, but no single approach stands out as the best way to deal with anxiety. Because anxiety may result from many causes or combinations of causes, management involves approaching the problem from several different perspectives.

Five different approaches—or a combination of approaches— may be used in anxiety management:

1. Utilize supportive therapy.

Use supportive therapy with every third-age client. This approach works best when the client is beset by fears about the future. Just knowing that someone is there can work wonders with such individuals. Let your client know that you understand the stress that they feel and that their stress is justified and a normal reaction. This alone may provide relief. Supplemental support with concrete actions to relieve stress may help the client deal with this demon called anxiety.

2. Consider the body.

Several factors increase or deter anxiety:

- Excessive consumption of caffeine (in coffee, tea, cola, or some medications) may increase anxiety levels. Caffeine is a stimulant and a person suffering from anxiety might consider decreasing or even eliminating consumption of stimulants.
- Foods containing the amino acid tryptophan may increase the level of the neurotransmitter serotonin, which is a calming chemical in the brain. Milk and turkey are both sources of tryptophan.
- Foods containing the amino acid tyrosine are thought to increase the levels in the brain of dopamine and epinephrine. These two substances appear to buffer the effects of stress. Fish and meat are sources of tyrosine.
- A high carbohydrate diet may exert an anti-anxiety effect.
- Some individuals have a "hyper" reaction to sugar.
- One of the most valuable aids in combating anxiety is exercise, especially aerobic exercise. Vigorous exercise produces chemical changes in the body that reduce anxiety and increase one's ability to deal with stress.

Review your client's dietary and lifestyle habits. If your anxious client tends to consume too much caffeine or sugar, a change in diet is necessary. If your client lives a sedentary life and could live more actively, exercise can be recommended. These changes may not eliminate the anxiety, but they can provide some relief.

3. Consider the mind.

Cognitive therapy can provide relief in dealing with the mental aspect of anxiety. Here you will attempt to examine and modify thoughts, beliefs, or assumptions that might increase or create anxiety. If your client is so fearful of what might happen he or she sits and worries incessantly about the future, try using relaxation tapes or practicing meditation (see Appendix 7).

4. Deal with lifestyle issues.

Some individuals have an innate tendency toward anxiety, although most people deal with this innate tendency relatively well. Encountering the array of third-age problems, some people's anxiety becomes more intense. What worked in earlier years may not work now. Edna was the bulwark of her five children for years, from when they were growing-up right on through their adulthood. Each time her children and grandchildren had a problem, they would go to her. After Edna entered her third age she started feeling guilty when she could not fix her family's problems. As a result, she suffered tremendous anxiety which turned into depression. Only when I persuaded the family to stop taking all their problems to her did Edna live more normally. In dealing with lifestyle anxiety, you may attempt to nudge the client into making certain lifestyle changes, either in approach or perception.

5. Use anti-anxiety medication.

Anti-anxiety medication such as Xanax and Ativan takes effect almost immediately, but it should be used to provide short-term relief—thirty days or less, for these drugs have a high dependence liability. (However, psychiatrists sometimes prescribe these drugs on a long-term maintenance basis in some situations.) When mild anxiety is a problem, anti-anxiety medication is as beneficial for its psychological effects as for its calming qualities. After all, anxiety is a condition created in the mind. By stressing how effective a specific medication can be over a period of a few weeks, clients sometimes respond to the belief that the medication will help them.

Dealing with anxiety often requires a multifaceted approach: reviewing the diet, prescribing certain psychological or lifestyle changes, providing supportive and cognitive therapies, and perhaps even suggesting medication. When anxiety has a multifaceted cause, it requires a multifaceted approach. An inherent tendency toward anxiety may be triggered by life-event crises. Not eating right and not exercising can magnify inherent-life event crises. If there are multiple causes treatment should encompass several approaches.

Case Studies

Martha

I became acquainted with Martha when a social worker from a long-term care institution referred her to me. Martha had been hospitalized with serious pulmonary and heart problems. She spent three weeks in intensive care and did not remember one moment of it. She then spent two months in rehabilitation in the long-term care facility, and although she was physically ready to return to her home, she could not bear to leave the security of her room.

When I visited Martha, I found a very anxious, highly sophisticated seventy-two-year-old woman who required oxygen twenty-four hours a day. (Her physician attributed the serious pulmonary problems to a lifetime of smoking.) Although she had no financial problems and could hire as much help as needed, she feared living a lifestyle in which she would always be hooked up to an oxygen tank.

A very organized person, Martha sat in her chair by her bed surrounded by brochures and notes that other people had given her. "I'm so confused by all this," she said. An independent and competent person, she now felt she had lost control of her life.

Martha had lost her first husband in World War II. A few years later she married a military man, and they spent twenty years living all over the country. When her husband retired and assumed an executive position at a local bank, Martha began teaching at the local college.

When I began working with Martha, her husband had died twelve years earlier. Her youngest son had died of AIDS five years earlier, and her remaining son lived two states away.

In working with Martha I kept in mind that people with pulmonary problems often suffer from anxiety and find it difficult to recover completely. I made arrangements for homecare services effective in two weeks when Martha was scheduled to return home. Setting a specific date seemed to provide her with the incentive she needed to return home. But after going home, she still felt extreme anxiety and feared being alone. While I used supportive therapy and some relaxation techniques with her, it seemed to me that her anxiety continued until it finally died out by itself. She regained a semblance of normality within about six weeks, although normality for Martha was quite different than it had been prior to her illness. To Martha, living a normal life now included leaving the house twice a week pulling an oxygen tank, having someone come in daily to help with household chores and meals, and a changed lifestyle. But she accepted this and lived comfortably with it.

John

John walked into a hospital emergency room complaining of panic attacks that seemed to have appeared with no reason. John was a verbal sixty-two-year old man who was very hyper and seemed mystified at the cause of his panic attacks. By the second session, I had discovered the underlying cause for John's anxiety: John, who was gay, was worrying about the health of Paul, his roommate of twelve years. Paul's physician feared that Paul might have cancer.

John and I tackled his anxiety using several approaches. After the first few sessions I decided that supportive therapy in itself would not help John deal with his anxiety. John's anxiety continued even after Paul learned that he did not have cancer. Cognitive therapy helped in part, but John calmed considerably when I realized how much caffeine he was consuming in a day and suggested a change. After John switched to decaffeinated coffee and caffeine-free cola, his anxiety dropped considerably. Although the panic attacks ceased, John's anxiety level remained higher than it had been prior to the attacks. We then arranged for the psychiatrist at the mental health center to prescribe an anti-anxiety medication, which in conjunction with the other approaches returned John's level of anxiety to what was normal for him.

Depression

Reactive or situational rather than chronic depression is a facet of almost every diagnosis of third-age clients. It usually has a concrete cause.

Third-age people with chronic depression, often the result of a chemical imbalance in the brain, have usually received antidepressants from their physician for much of their lives. Although chronic depression may befall individuals for the first time when they enter their third age, most often it is situational, a reaction to life experiences such as a serious loss, chronic illness, economic problems, or difficulty in relationships. These experiences can also happen to a person who has had depressive tendencies throughout life. The combination of a depressive tendency and a situational trauma throws the individual into depression.

Depression can be devastating. A whole person illness that affects thoughts, mood, body, and lifestyle, treatment through counseling and medication helps an estimated 80 percent of those afflicted. The problem is that an estimated 85 percent of third-age people with depression do not seek treatment. Among the reasons for this are:

- Some people fail to recognize the symptoms of depression.
- Other people assume that depression or feeling blue is an inherent part of the aging process.
- Sometimes a person who has health problems or who has suffered other losses assumes that depression normally accompanies the problem.
- Many individuals simply do not wish to ask for counseling or emotional support.
- Some individuals continue to view seeking counseling or asking for medication from a physician as a sign of weakness.
- Some individuals avoid treatment because of the cost involved. (If no community mental health is available, the cost of private counselors exceeds many Social Security budgets.)

For these reasons as well as others, depression, which is a treatable disease, often goes untreated.

Symptoms of Depression

Most people experience times in their lives when they feel blue or generally unhappy. But when this feeling persists for a couple of weeks or when interest is lost in formerly pleasurable activities, a person may be suffering from depression. Here are a few symptoms that may be present when a person is depressed:

- Increase or decrease in appetite.

- Changes in sleeping patterns—sleeping more or sleeping less.
- Increase or decrease in activities.
- Fatigue or loss of energy.
- Irritability.
- Inability to concentrate.
- Feelings of worthlessness.
- Feelings of excessive guilt.
- Thoughts of death or suicide, and sometimes attempts at suicide.
- Feelings of hopelessness, pessimism.
- Difficulty concentrating, remembering, making decisions.
- Persistent physical symptoms such as headaches, digestive disorders, and chronic pain that do not respond to treatment.
- General confusion.

When depression is severe enough, especially in third-age people, it may resemble dementia. Normally, when depression is situational, it follows a major life crisis. The crisis may be the loss of a significant person or a physical loss, such as loss of mobility, hearing, vision, or any aspect of life that has meaning for a person. Depression may also be a side effect of medication: some commonly used drugs that sometimes cause depressive symptoms include steroids, some heart medicines, some high blood pressure medications, and combinations of other medicines that interact antagonistically with each other. Depression may appear in conjunction with some physical problems: endocrine diseases, heart disease, neurological problems, infections, malignancies, and vitamin deficiencies.

Dealing with Depression

Most of the clients who come to you for help will be suffering from reactive or situational depression. On occasion you will see a client with depressive tendencies who has suffered from a lifetime of "feeling blue," although this person may never have been treated. With such a client, medication becomes almost a necessity, for more than likely your client's depression results from a chemical imbalance. Counseling can help him or her with this affliction, but medication is almost a requirement.

The following approaches are appropriate treatments for clients suffering from reactive or situational depression:

1. Counseling

With a depressed client, I use a combination of supportive and cognitive therapies, with the mix varying according to the client. When dealing with a client who is more aware, more rational, and more sophisticated, I prefer to begin with supportive therapy and then in time I adopt some aspects of cognitive therapy. Sometimes a client is too devastated or too unsophisticated for cognitive therapy. When a client appears to be suffering from a situational or reactive depression, I prefer to use a mini-analysis approach. I spend a couple of sessions discussing the client's growing-up years and general lifestyle prior to the event or situation that appears responsible for the depression. Not only does this approach provide information about the client, but it also helps establish rapport and encourages the client to become more introspective. After these background sessions, your client will reach a point where he or she is ready to discuss the specific event or situation that has, at least in part, created the depression. From this point, you and your client may work specifically on various aspects of the causative situation—what life was like prior to this event, the event itself, the changes resulting from the event, the pressures resulting from the changes, and how he or she might better deal with these pressures.

Always remember that each situation is different from a previous situation. Clients, especially third-age clients, have different strengths and limitations, and you must adjust to each unique situation.

2. Medication

Should you determine that your client would benefit from medication, in addition to persuading him or her to consider an antidepressant, you must have a source for this medication. The client who comes to a counselor for help may already be taking medication prescribed by a family physician. Ideally, all psychotropic medication should be prescribed by psychiatrists. This is their specialty and they are aware of options, dosages, and possible adverse reactions of combinations of different medications. (Many third-age people take several medications.) Family physicians are generalists who know comparatively little about psychotropic medications: they sometimes prescribe the wrong medication or the wrong dosage for the situation. When you believe a client would benefit from medication, suggest a medication appointment with the mental health center psychiatrist, or a doctor you trust. If your client is already taking medication prescribed by a family physician, check it out informally with the psychiatrist. If the medication is inappropriate, urge the client to consider a medication appointment with the psychiatrist. Most family physicians are cautious about prescribing psychotropic medication, never going beyond a mild antidepressant or anti-anxiety medication.

In general, physicians or psychiatrists will prescribe three major antidepressants: Tricyclics, for poor appetite and sleeplessness; MAO inhibitors, for increased appetite and/or sleeping; Lithium for repeated episodes of depression.

Some medications have side effects—a client may have a reaction to the specific medication or to a combination of medications. It is important that a prescriber have a list of all medications the client is ingesting and monitor the client if the medication is to be continued for an extended period. Monitoring can be difficult with clients who have a lackadaisical perspective toward medication.

Even if a client would benefit from a medication, sometimes a physician or psychiatrist will not prescribe it because of age and living conditions. Age in itself usually does not preclude a client from receiving medication. However, if the client is what is sometimes called the frail elderly and lives alone, prescribers sometimes are hesitant about giving prescriptions. The major consideration is whether the client can be trusted to ingest a medication as prescribed and whether that medication will negatively affect the client's body or mind. As a person ages, the body changes and tolerances and reactions change. When asked how he prescribed medication for elderly clients, a physician at a workshop I attended responded with two words: "Very carefully."

3. Counseling and Medication

Mental health professionals and physicians have different attitudes about the mix of counseling and medication. Some rely primarily on medications; others use medication only as a last resort, which is my personal preference. If my client appears to have had depressive tendencies throughout life, then I will suggest medication appropriate to his or her age and lifestyle. If my client seems to be reacting to an event or having difficulty adjusting to a new lifestyle, then I will suggest medication only if counseling does not seem to accomplish our goals. Sometimes medication provides a boost that allows counseling to work more effectively.

When dealing with a client suffering from depression, remember that much of the time the depression is a symptom not a cause. You must deal not only with the depression but with what causes the depression, and you must determine the source of the depression and how to deal with it on an individual basis.

Case Studies

Josephine

When Josephine entered my office for the first time, she did not strike me as being unusual in any way. She was suffering from depression, although the depression was only a symptom of deeper problems.

She had placed her husband, dead twelve years, on the world's tallest pedestal. She remembered only the good things about her life with him; however, as she served me tidbits of her life, I saw that he'd had his limitations. Josephine's perception of her good life had ended the day George died. She desperately wanted a good relationship with her only child, a daughter of fifty. Wanda cared little about her mother, took advantage of Josephine, and seemed to build her life around her alcoholic third husband from whom she was divorced. Because of her dissatisfaction with her life without George and her inability to establish a satisfactory relationship with Wanda, instead of turning to alcohol Josephine had turned to credit cards. She owed various credit card companies a total of $6,000.

Josephine had been on an antidepressant for several years to little effect, so counseling would have to cure her depression, which I felt resulted primarily from disappointments in her life. I arranged for her to visit a credit counselor, who convinced her to destroy all but one credit card and arranged for her to pay off her $6,000 at a rate of about $200 a month. (Although the companies did not like this approach and continued sending Josephine nasty letters, the financial counselor made them accept the formula. Under this plan, Josephine would have her bills paid off in four years.) I helped her realize that she could not build her life around Wanda , who obviously would never provide her with the kind of devotion and attention that she wanted.

I worked with Josephine weekly for about four months. For the first three months, I used general supportive therapy with her, simply allowing her to talk and "nudging" her into some understanding about her credit card addiction and her difficulties with her daughter. In the final month, we worked with a variety of cognitive techniques to help her build a rational perception of herself and the world. Although Josephine achieved real success, even today she comes in every couple of months for a kind of booster shot. She is a perfect example of the client whose depression is little more than a symptom of other underlying problems, not all of which can be solved.

Carl

When Carl got out of the army many years ago, he married a woman seventeen years his senior. They ignored the age difference, had four children and completely enjoyed one another. Carl worked and Lucille kept house. When Carl reached the age of sixty-five, he retired.

A year later, disaster struck. At the age of eighty-three, Lucille had a devastating stroke, that left her totally paralyzed on one side. Her disability was such that Carl was forced to place her in a nursing home. He had tried to care for her at home, but after two weeks he realized that he and his adult children could not provide the care she needed.

Carl did not adjust well to this new lifestyle. Twice a day he drove over to the nursing home to see Lucille and help her with her meals. He had three concerns: he could not stand living in the small house the couple had bought six years ago; he did not like being alone; and he had difficulty handling money—Lucille had always done that.

At the prompting of his physician, Carl called the mental health center. He sounded calm on the telephone, but when I visited his home that afternoon, I found him still dressed in pajamas and robe though it was three-thirty. Carl quickly unburdened himself. After explaining what had happened in his life, he shook his head. "If I had a goddamned shotgun, I'd shoot myself," he said, "I really would ."

I believed him. Carl was a classic example of a man simultaneously anxious and depressed. He could not deal with his situation, and I decided that I could most effectively help him by helping him change his life. Carl needed to see that his life could continue. After talking with him an hour, we made a list of things he wanted to do. He had already accepted that his wife would spend the rest of her life in a nursing home, and that she might live two weeks or five years. Now he wanted to get out of the house. "I can't stand living here," he told me. "Everywhere I turn, I see my wife."

He needed help with his finances. "I get these bills through the mail. I pay the lights and water and throw the rest of the bills away. A damned credit card company keeps calling me all the time."

He could not stand being alone. "I'm not good at being alone," he said.

We spent the next two months changing his life to one he could tolerate. In many ways, Carl was nearly helpless, but he could not ask for much help from his adult children. I was concerned about helping Carl make too many changes too fast, but he was determined to change his life.

Working together, we got his finances in order. I wrote or called all his creditors and arranged a different payment plan. His credit card company talked tough—at least for a while but when I explained that Carl was potentially suicidal, the company went along with our plan to pay the principal with no interest charges.

I helped Carl move into a high-rise, seniors-only apartment building. Carl had wanted to simply walk off and leave his house, but at my suggestion he informed his adult children of his plans. One of his daughters assumed the loan and moved in.

Once the pressure had been removed, Carl stopped talking about suicide and started caring about living. In the high-rise, he developed a routine of having coffee with the boys, seeing his wife, eating lunch at the high-rise, seeing his wife, eating dinner out, and returning to his efficiency apartment in the evening. "Why, I'm so busy I don't have time to think bad thoughts," he said.

Abnormal Grief

Perhaps the most difficult challenge facing third-age people is adjusting to the loss of significant people in their lives. Even when a normal adjustment is possible, it's still painful. If a person does not adjust normally, life becomes almost unbearable. Sometimes an inability to deal with grief results in premature death for the remaining spouse or parent.

Considerable progress was made in understanding grief when researchers defined the stages of mourning. Although different individuals describe these stages somewhat differently, a person who deals with grief must:

- Accept the reality of the loss

Because the death of a loved one creates profound sorrow, some people may refuse to accept the reality of the loss. Those who do not accept this reality have delusions about the deceased. He or she may search crowds for a glimpse of the deceased or even imagine being visited by that person.

This reaction is normal, at least for awhile. But the reaction becomes abnormal when people react as Queen Victoria did after Prince Albert died. She had his clothes and shaving gear laid out daily as if he were alive, and she walked around the palace speaking to him. Some mourners can intellectually accept that someone is dead and will not return, but emotionally they may have difficulty accepting that reality.

- Experience the pain of grief

A survivor must experience the pain of grief to move past it. When a person experiences a loss but feels no pain, that survivor may have short-circuited the pain by denying or ignoring the loss. Often, the person merely postpones dealing with the grief, and this postponement may result in depression. In our culture viewing the body and participating in a memorial service is part of the grief process. When circumstances deny these rituals to survivors, the grief process may be blocked. Although I question the value of viewing the body, because I see no therapeutic benefit in looking at a body that has been ravaged by cancer or disease, a memorial service of some sort is necessary for closure. Many people require a formal announcement that a life has ended and that those who remain must continue living.

- Adjust to an environment in which the deceased is missing

Although the grieving process requires two to four years, and never ends for some people, after approximately three months a survivor realizes that the deceased is gone and will never return. The survivor adjusts his or her lifestyle and goes on with life. For example, people who are married for long periods, assume certain roles and certain duties. When half of a partnership disappears, the survivor must assume all the roles. The adjustment process can be more difficult when a survivor must learn totally new skills and new roles.

- Withdraw emotional energy from the old relationship and re-invest it in another relationship or other activities

After a year or so, a survivor begins severing the emotional bond with a deceased person and becomes interested in other people or other activities. A person may feel guilty when this process begins, but this change in emotional energy does not mean the deceased person is forgotten. It just means that the survivor is moving on. Sometimes a survivor needs permission to pursue new emotional ties. Two years after Ted lost his wife, his nephew wrote suggesting Ted begin looking around. Although he never remarried, Ted thanked his nephew profusely for this permission. After a loss, individuals who have no interest in seeking a new relationship still need the same sort of healing, or permission, to continue living a viable life.

Intensity of Grief

Grief's intensity varies among individuals for several reasons. Most people can deal with the passing of a neighbor or an acquaintance without difficulty. There may be sadness, but after a few days they return to normal life. But when there is a strong attachment to a spouse, child, or even close friend, that death is felt intensely. The type of relationship is a factor in the degree of grieving. If a wife loses a husband on whom she has been very dependent, she must not only adjust to that loss, but she also must establish a new life in which the responsibility for decisions is hers alone.

Cause of death can be natural, accidental, suicidal, or homicidal and each affects the grief process of a survivor differently. Generally speaking, sudden deaths are more difficult to deal with than expected deaths, which usually occur as a result of an illness, and are anticipated. Accidental deaths, suicides, and homicides occur without warning, although natural deaths from heart disease and similar causes also can occur without warning. What affects people most are deaths that seem senseless or premature. A senseless death may leave a survivor feeling guilty and wondering if that senseless death could have been prevented. The loss is magnified if the death is premature. Perhaps the most difficult death to deal with involves a child senselessly murdered, because parents do not expect to outlive their children.

Successfully dealing with a loss depends in part upon the strength and stability of the survivor. A strong, secure person will find a way to deal with a loss no matter how difficult. An insecure, fragile, or anxiety-ridden person has more difficulty adjusting to the loss of a significant person, especially in the absence of an extensive support system. If a fragile survivor has no support system, dealing with a loss becomes more difficult. If a fragile survivor has a strong support system, a loss can be manageable.

Helping Clients Deal with Abnormal Grief

When a client is having difficulty dealing with grief, I assume the person has had difficulty dealing with many other crises in life. I generally receive these referrals when six months or more have passed and a survivor is showing no sign of dealing effectively with the loss. In helping a survivor deal with the grief process:

1. Use supportive therapy primarily.

Although medication and some cognitive therapy may be appropriate with some grieving clients, supportive therapy is the treatment of choice. Despite the degree of instability or fragility involved, the client must work through the grief process. The client must feel that the grieving process is reasonably complete before a semblance of normality is regained. The best healers are support and time.

2. Assist with attaining independence.

When a grief stricken client has difficulty dealing with a problem, the major obstacle to resolution may be the fear of living independently. This happens with women who have lost husbands who basically took care of them; however, third-age men have more difficulty dealing with grief than do women because they depended almost completely on wives for friendship and emotional support, whereas women typically receive support from other women. After losing a spouse, men often remarry within a couple of years.

3. Help remove barriers to recovery.

Consciously or unconsciously, survivors may place barriers to obstruct the grief process. Some believe that a long period of grief is a sign of love. Even when a survivor is ready for the grief process to end, an adult child or children may demand that the survivor remain pure for the memory of dear old dad or dear old mom. There may be secondary gains from playing the role of the grieving spouse or the grieving parent, such as more admiration or attention from adult children, friends, and neighbors.

4. Conduct an informal life review.

Conducting a life review with third-age clients is a technique that has been used for many years and has proven to be a valuable tool for many situations. When grief is a problem, encourage your client to discuss the life that he or she had with the deceased. If the deceased happens to be a son, daughter, father, or mother, conduct a family life review. If the deceased is a spouse, I conduct a marital life review. But regardless of the focus of a life review, the purpose is to encourage the client to talk about the deceased, about himself or herself, and about life without the deceased.

Consoling the Client

Your observation or a communicated thought may provide the means for your client to understand what has happened. After a loss, your client may face what appears to be an impossible situation. Many clients have told me, "I could never do that" only to then do what they considered impossible. The following tidbits of wisdom might come in handy in helping clients gain insight or new perspectives:

- Grief is the price we pay for loving.

It hurts terribly to lose a parent, a sibling, a spouse, an adult child, a close friend. But consider the alternative. Who would be content not having someone to love? So, despite the difficulty encountered over loss, be thankful that there are people to love. Grief is a trade-off: for all the good years with your loved one before the loss.

- To bury grief, take little steps forward.

Working through the grief process requires time. The tremendous shock we feel when someone close dies may feel like losing part of ourselves. The suffering will end only if it is worked at. A switch cannot be flipped to end the suffering; rather, we move forward tentatively, one step at a time; slowly, gently.

- The laws of nature do not protect good people.

Neither a bullet nor a malignant tumor has a conscience. Sometimes life is fair, and sometimes it is grossly unfair. When the grossly unfair happens, don't waste time seeking the reason it happened; deal with it. Work at it. Take little steps forward.

- Vulnerability to death is one of life's conditions.

Life is a trade-off. To live, one must die. Ideally, the trade-off works this way: there is birth; a tremendously rewarding life, and death at ninety-five after the body has worn out. Some people live this idyllic life; others are born with genetic predispositions that prevent an idyllic life. But regardless of whether one lives an idyllic life or experiences problems, everyone must die. Watching a significant person die a premature death is probably life's greatest hurt. Most people do not fear death as much as they fear premature death—either for themselves or for others.

When a significant person is struck down in the second, third, fourth, fifth or even sixth decade of life, the loss is felt deeper. The grief is not only because that person will no longer participate in life, but also because of the time that person has lost, and the experiences the person will never have. It seems unfair. It is unfair.

- After living through the death of a loved one, we fear our own future less.

With each significant loss a part of us dies a little. Granted, we recover and live again, but a part of ourselves is buried. If life is exceptionally cruel and significant losses are suffered too soon, it can become an almost unbearable burden. Sometimes people begin thinking about what life really means and they realize that jobs and cars and houses have little meaning. Terminally ill people often experience their most significant insights in the limited time left to them. After standing by a significant person with a terminal illness, most survivors lose some fear of the future—nothing could be as devastating as the experience they have just survived.

- The world would not survive if everyone lived forever.

When a significant person is lost to premature death, we may think, "If only she had another decade." But in a way, time is irrelevant. If humans had evolved to the point where we lived a thousand or five thousand years, there would still be grief at premature death.

Imagine the problem that would develop if people lived forever. More than likely, people would stop having children. Life is a process, a trade-off: we live and we die.

- Because people have free will, they sometimes hurt one another.

People hurt one another in the course of pursuing their own goals or lifestyle choices, in retribution, by what is not done, or by accident. In a way, when a significant person dies, he or she hurts us by leaving, by no longer participating in our life. When the death is premature, suicide, by driving too fast, having a heart that wore out, or even by being a victim of fate, we have difficulty in living with the pain.

- Try not to blame yourself.

When a significant person dies, there is an inevitable search for an explanation, and much of the time there is self-blame. "If only I had..." Sometimes it helps to realize that the world does not make sense. People are human, people make mistakes, but most of the time what happened would have happened no matter what action we might have taken.

What happens after we have lost a significant person?

We grieve, go through hell, do some soul-searching, and, ultimately, go on living. We concern ourselves with how we responded to the death and what we intend to do now that it has happened, now that life has changed. We choose whether to continue living or to spend the rest of our lives grieving. The choice is ours.

Case Studies

Charlotte

Seventy-five-year-old Charlotte had an unbelievably difficult time adjusting to the loss of her husband of fifty years. They had been a conventional blue collar couple. Max had worked at a small factory, and Charlotte had spent her life in the caretaker role. They had no children. They lived a very sheltered life; only once in fifty years had she left the small city where they lived. After her husband retired they ventured out of the house to buy groceries and eat breakfast each morning at a fast food restaurant. They spent the rest of the time indoors. Charlotte had no major health problems but she was overweight. She spent most of her time sitting in a chair in front of the television, and she could barely walk. During the time that I knew her, she fell several times.

When I first began seeing her, I assumed that Max had died just a short time previously. However, I discovered in the second session that Max had died almost two years ago. Charlotte was stuck in stage one of the grief process, and I had my hands full trying to help her continue with life. She would not even begin to help herself. All she wanted to do was sit in her chair, which was right beside the chair where her husband had sat, and watch television shows.

Her major concern was that her husband didn't talk to her anymore. "He used to come and see me every night," she said. "He would talk to me. Now he doesn't talk to me any more." That she believed her dead husband visited her did not concern me, for these visits were decreasing in intensity and I believed the visits would end.

In time, Charlotte accepted the death of her husband. His imagined visits ceased. But she did not care enough about life without her husband to create a new life. She would not abandon her chair or the symbolic chair beside hers. A counselor cannot reconstruct a life without a client's help.

Betty

Seventy-two-year-old Betty was in many ways Charlotte's mirror image. Both were wives of retired factory workers. Both depended greatly on their husbands. Both had spent their lives as homemakers. But there were differences. Although Betty had a host of health problems, including diabetes and heart disease, she worked at creating a new life, whereas Charlotte had just sat and vegetated. After her husband died, Betty and a girlfriend drove to Florida to spend the winter in her travel trailer. Unfortunately, the few months in Florida brought disaster, in the form of illnesses to both of them. Betty limped back home and called me immediately.

After she listed all the problems she and her friend had encountered in Florida, she shook her head. "To live down there you need a man around. If Dad had been down there with me, none of that would have happened. Dad, he could fix anything." Betty was able to reach a semblance of normalcy after four months, although she had not yet completed her grieving process. Charlotte simply sat and allowed social service agencies to care for her, Betty continued working at rebuilding her life.

Chapter 6

Retirement and Independent Living

Retirement

Some people spend their lives preparing for retirement. They develop hobbies and interests; they love to travel and go south in the winter or wherever their fancy leads them. When they reach the third age, people in this group spend ten to forty delightful years in leisure. Where they had worked only to live, others had lived to work. Those who lived to work may have difficulty adjusting to retirement, difficulty adjusting to life without work. My father spent most of his working life as a farmer. When he was sixty-two, the farm on which he had lived and worked for thirty-five years was sold. He and my mother bought a small home in a nearby town and "retired." After a year, he could deal with the enforced idleness no longer. "I don't like this stayin' home all the time," he said. He was not suited for retirement. He would not drink coffee with the boys. He had no hobbies. All he did for a year was sit in a chair, watch television, and drive my mother batty with his dissatisfaction.

Then an opportunity arose for him to work as a delivery man at an office supply store. He literally jumped at this opportunity, and he is still delivering office supplies at eighty. Perhaps the greatest fear of his life, other than losing my mother, is that some day he will no longer be able to work. At first he would begin work at the store at 8 a.m., then he gradually began to arrive at work earlier and earlier. Today he reaches the store at 6 a.m., charts out his delivery plan for the day, and spends the day making forty to fifty deliveries. A gregarious sort, he enjoys meeting people, and people along his route call him "Pops."

What are the pressures that can make retirement a time of hell rather than a time of pleasure? Your client may cite one of the following scenarios:

- There's nothing to do with the time.

Some individuals never develop interests in life outside of work. They work five days a and relax in the evenings. When the weekend arrives, they do chores and errands on Saturday and relax on Sunday. When time comes for them to retire, they have nothing to do. Retirement in general is more difficult for men than women—although that may change as more women devote their lives to careers—because traditional women who spend their time caring for husbands and family often find their life changes very little: they continue caring for their husbands, only now they are home all the time.

- Nothing exciting happens.

To some people, jobs offer stimulation. Being with interesting people, being motivated to complete specific tasks, working under deadlines. Retirement may not offer replacement stimulation, and they become bored. Again, this happens more often with men because women have often led more varied lifestyles. Also, because women work awhile, remain home with children awhile, and then return to work, The variety of life experiences helps women adapt more easily to changes inherent in retirement. Single people—whether never married, divorced, or widowed—may miss the workplace more than anyone else. The workplace was where they associated with acquaintances and friends. A person who has made little effort to create a circle of friends outside the workplace may end up sitting alone in an apartment. Some people adapt to this new situation and broaden their social circle; others merely sit.

- My spouse is driving me crazy.

Serious marital problems develop when a couple cannot adjust to different roles and to different lifestyle situations after retirement. Over a lifetime, couples adopt a division of labor. A wife, whether or not she works outside the home, performs certain functions and a husband performs others. They also spend their leisure time in specific ways. They may attend sporting events, participate in church activities, or spend their leisure time in any of a thousand ways. When retirement disrupts this division of labor difficulties may result.

Helping Clients Adjust to Retirement

As a counselor you can help clients who are having difficulty adjusting to retirement, by evaluating how your clients spend their time. Obvious suggestions for increased involvement in life include volunteering, working part-time, traveling, developing a hobby, returning to school, and so on. However, you can only make suggestions and hope that your client will examine the opportunities for spending leisure time.

When people think of volunteering, their vision often stops with the local hospital. There are literally thousands of governmental and private agencies that need extra help. A bored, retired mechanic might become involved with a local senior center in repairing cars for people with little money. Work with your client to brainstorm opportunities for spending leisure time.

You can also work with your client to change his or her perspective. When people have difficulty adjusting to retirement, a loss of self esteem often accompanies the boredom. Almost anytime people become unhappy, they begin to wonder about their value. Use cognitive therapy to rebuild a client's self image. This rebuilding process can be accomplished with a life review, an appreciation of the person's strengths, and the use of other standard cognitive therapy techniques.

Although most people adjust to retirement reasonably well, this adjustment often requires at least two years. When dealing with a client who has difficulty adjusting to retirement, offer alternative ways of spending time and help rebuild the client's self image. How far the client ultimately progresses depends upon his or her motivation.

Case Studies

Marge

Marge had never been a happy person. She grew up in an unusual family arrangement. After her father died when she was a few years old, she and her mother Rachel went to live with Rachel's family, a family that included a grandmother, two uncles, and an aunt, all of whom lived together in a large farm house. Of the siblings, only Rachel had married, and her silent, work-oriented brothers and sisters dominated her. As a result, Marge grew up in a family of adults, all of whom found fault with Marge and attempted to mold her into their image.

Marge married early, primarily to escape her home. She was a homemaker for the next thirty years and reared three children. Her husband Edward became successful in the corporation where he worked, but he was difficult for Marge and their children to live with. Not only was Edward a workaholic who spent fifty hours a week at the corporation, he drank heavily. A cold, emotionally cruel man, Edward lived his own life, paying little attention to his wife and children. Then he began having an affair with a woman twenty years younger than Marge. He divorced Marge to live with his new love, whom he married two weeks after the divorce was final.

Marge was now alone. Her husband was gone, her children had left home. At age forty-seven she began a new life. After moping for awhile, she enrolled in the first displaced homemaker's course at a local community college. She earned an associate degree in secretarial science, got a job, then focused her life on her job. She remained in that same job for nineteen years, retiring only when she had eye problems.

But Marge was not happy in retirement. Her life had no focus. Rather than being deeply depressed, she lived a dull, meaningless life that left her unsatisfied.

When she came to see me, I quickly realized that she was going to be a difficult case. Not only was she living the dull ache of a retirement, but she also kept denying the existence of the extra baggage that she carried with her. Marge required a bit of problem-solving, some probing and talking about the past, a bit of cognitive therapy aimed at changing her perspective, and a mild antidepressant that hopefully would lift her mood while we were working on the other aspects of treatment.

Marge erected roadblocks at every suggestion. She refused to discuss her past. She had no interest in participating in some of the cognitive therapy techniques. She said her health would not allow her to volunteer. She said she did not like to take medication. What Marge wanted was a magic pill that would instantly change her life.

Three months after our first contact, as tactfully as I could, I explained that although I had been searching for it, I had found no magic pill. I explained that I believed I could help her but this help would require time, effort, and cooperation on her part. "I want to think about it," she said. I never saw her again. As far as I know, she continues to brood miserably in her apartment.

Fred

Fred spent his life as a successful salesman, driving all over the midwestern United States, selling office equipment to mid-sized companies. A jovial man who enjoyed people, he knew by name all the people in the offices of his clients. He enjoyed selling and he was good at it. He retired at seventy, only when age forced him to give up life on the road and when his wife's health began to deteriorate.

Because he had saved his money, he had no economic woes. His original plan was to buy a motor home and drive around the country visiting places and talking to people. And, he and his wife Amy had lived this lifestyle for awhile. However, Amy's continuing health problems ended this pleasurable activity, for which Fred was well suited. He then tried volunteer work but didn't really like this activity. "I feel like an errand boy," was how he described his volunteer work at a local hospital.

"I need something to do," he said, after a friend of his with whom I had worked suggested he call me. As he explained his situation, I began thinking of a way to help Fred. It was a problem-solving situation. Fred did not need counseling.

Each morning I buy a copy of *The New York Times* and read it during the day. When I am out making home visits, I stop at a fast food restaurant for fifteen minutes, drink coffee and read *The Times*. Some of the McDonald's and Hardee's employ third-age people to wipe off the tables and pour coffee. Since economics was not a need, I suggested that Fred might inquire into this kind of job. "I'll think about it," Fred replied.

Two weeks later I stopped at a McDonald's to do some serious newspaper reading and coffee drinking. "Hi, pardner," I heard a voice say. There was Fred, dressed in a McDonald's uniform, dish cloth in one hand and coffeepot in the other. "I love this job," he said. "Hell, I'd even pay them to do it." That was almost two years ago. Fred still works three mornings a week at the same McDonald's. He also comes in one afternoon a week to call bingo.

I see Fred about once a week when I go into that McDonald's. I hear Fred's jovial, "Hi, pardner," and never have to worry about a refill.

Independent Living

When I first began working with third-age people, I was amazed at the services available to help them remain independent in their homes. In the midwestern city where I work, private and public agencies and groups almost step on one another in their attempt to provide services. Although some duplication of services exists, the funds allocated for these services save taxpayers billions of dollars. Because nursing homes cost of $2,000 to $4,000 a month, most people who enter a nursing home use up their assets in less than a year. Their nursing home bills are then paid by Medicaid, which of course is paid by the government. From a purely economic perspective, money spent to help people remain independent is a bargain for taxpayers.

Independence and the Frail Years

When people enter their frail years, remaining independent becomes a problem. Some people remain independent until the last few months of their lives, while others who have difficulty coping may give up independence quickly or easily. Sometimes this results from physical problems, sometimes from attitude problems. To different people, the frail years provide different options.

1. Living in another's care.

Nursing homes are filled with people who are totally dependent on others. About half of the nursing home population suffers from dementia—Alzheimer's disease and the like—while the other half cannot, or believe they cannot, care for themselves. Some must deal with disease; others have weak, infirm bodies that have almost stopped functioning; still others simply have lost the will to live and have gone to a nursing home to die.

2. Living with some assistance.

Far less public or private money is required to live independently than to live in a nursing home. The assistance required to maintain an independent lifestyle may come from family, caring individuals, private organizations, government or government supported agencies. Some people in their frail years live with family, in group homes, or in retirement homes in which each resident has a small apartment but may eat in a community dining room if desired. Others live in their own home or apartment with assistance from human service organizations. Meals on Wheels, for example, may provide a hot lunch. A housekeeper may perform chores a person can no longer do. In-home assistance is perhaps the most valuable commodity to people in their frail years, for it allows many individuals to remain independent.

3. Totally caring for one's needs.

Not everyone possesses the will, the health, or the stamina to live alone to great age. For those who do, the major advantage to living independently is it forces a person to remain active. While living at any age requires effort, activity is more important for those over eighty. In fact, living independently may in itself be life sustaining.

The greatest danger for those in their frail years is *not* the possibility of suffering a heart attack, falling on ice, or being mugged in a park, but succumbing to complete dependence. Lottie was the eighty-six-year-old mother of four who, although somewhat crippled by arthritis, was in good health. Her three daughters, all of whom lived in the same geographic area, persuaded Lottie to leave the large family home and move into a small apartment. The daughters then proceeded to take turns caring for her. "They babied her to death," her son told me. "Mom kind of gave up and let them take care of her. But when she became more feeble, they realized what they were doing. So they stayed away more and let Mom take care of herself most of the time. She got better."

People in their frail years may grow so physically weak from inactivity that they become near invalids. A woman who was referred to our agency was described as confused, but after talking with her I found her to be a mentally alert woman in her early seventies with no major health problems. However, her major exertion consisted of moving from bed to couch. Her infirmity resulted from inactivity. My counseling consisted of involving her in a walking program to help her regain her strength.

In many ways, living the frail years resembles living in any other stage of life. One tries to control life rather than allowing life to control him or her. One option is to succumb, to allow one's body to become so weak and infirm that moving merely from bed to couch requires great effort. The other option is to challenge directly the onslaught of age, to strive to remain active and independent.

Supportive and Cognitive Therapy

Working with people who live independently and want to remain independent involves using supportive and cognitive therapy, arranging for services, and working with the family.

When a person trying to remain independent has problems, symptoms of anxiety and/or depression may appear. In many instances, time and supportive therapy will suffice. In some situations, cognitive therapy may provide greater benefits, but supportive therapy functions as the primary vehicle, for support is usually what the client in this situation needs most. Stress that your client can remain independent, then help him or her obtain any necessary services.

For some clients to remain independent, case management services are required. Assess your client's needs and arrange for services. Other social agencies may have arranged services, but check to see your client has chore housekeeper services to clean on a weekly basis and do grocery shopping and transportation to and from physicians' offices. Although you may make any of these arrangements, encourage your client to personally arrange services if possible. It is important that your clients feel in control of their lives to the greatest possible extent.

Working with a family often becomes an integral part of helping your client remain independent. With many third-age clients, a counselor never meets the family, but when independence is an issue, the family becomes involved.

Case Studies

Margaret

A teacher in Wisconsin named Oscar called to tell me that his recently widowed mother was having difficulty remaining independent. Oscar had called every social service agency in the city until one referred him to our program. We talked and then I visited his mother Margaret. She lived in a nice home in a well-to-do section of the city. Margaret was a tiny, frail-looking woman of sixty-eight who suffered from a multiple sclerosis-like disease. Margaret used a walker to maneuver around her home. She was very anxious, and was having great difficulty dealing with the death of her husband Alexander who had passed away six months earlier.

Margaret had suffered from her progressive muscular disease since high school. Now she could barely move even with the help of a walker. Despite her illness, she had married, stayed at home in the role of homemaker, and raised three children, who were now scattered to different parts of the country. To a great degree, Alexander had dominated Margaret's life. However, he had done this in a protective, gentle sort of way, made a better than average income as a small businessman, and they had lived a good life together.

After Alexander had died unexpectedly of a heart attack, Margaret experienced many difficulties dealing with life. Not only did she have difficulties dealing with her grief, but she also had problems simply living. Some of her problems resulted from her disability but others resulted from her dependence on her husband. When I began working with her, she was depressed, anxious, and not coping at all with life.

For three months I worked with Margaret in weekly sessions helping her to deal with grief and her symptoms of anxiety and depression. I helped her to continue living independently and manage her own affairs. The biggest challenge was to coax her into doing things by herself.

This was a slow process. But Mary gradually changed her mindset from "my-husband-will-do-it-for-me" to "I've-got-to-do-it-myself." One afternoon I received another call from Oscar. Her ecstatic son called from Wisconsin to say, "I talked to my mother last night. She told me she had called a taxi and gone to the dentist—by herself!"

Oscar was shocked because he did not remember his mother ever doing anything for herself, let alone living independently not long after the death of her husband. Margaret reminded me of a small child just learning to walk: after that first step, she gained confidence with every step.

Marva

I was in a meeting one afternoon when a co-worker knocked on the door and motioned for me to come out. "You have a problem in your office." In my office I found Beth so angry with her mother, Marva, that she was almost at the point of abuse.

Marva was a tiny woman of sixty-eight who weighed maybe eighty pounds. Born and raised in Kentucky, Marva had lost none of her country affectations. She and her husband Reuben had eight children before he died of lung cancer and alcoholism a decade ago, and since that time Marva had lived with relatives, dependent on them for support. She would stay with a sibling or an adult child for awhile, and then the relative would pass Marva along to another family member. She had recently lived with a brother in Kentucky. When the brother could no longer stand the situation, he put her on a bus and shipped her to Beth, who was the youngest daughter. Although she lived in her own small apartment, Marva had recently begun having panic attacks. At the hint of an attack, she would call Beth and demand that someone come and get her. Since this happened several times a week, Beth was rapidly becoming impatient with her mother and feared that her mother would be unable to remain independent.

I began visiting Marva a couple of times a week, providing support and establishing rapport. In time, Marva explained that her panic attacks occurred only when she was alone in her apartment. She felt these attacks occurred because she lived in a basement apartment with the windows so high that she could not see out.

As I talked with Marva, I became convinced that there was no reason for her not to live independently for many more years. Her health seemed good and she had good mobility. So I suggested that she apply for an apartment in a high-rise where she would have her own apartment as well as be among people. In discussing this, I also subtly pointed out that this would allow her to avoid bothering Beth. Marva admitted that she knew Beth was impatient and frustrated because of all the calls.

Both Marva and Beth enthusiastically endorsed the idea of Marva living in a high-rise. Because Marva would have to wait three months for an apartment, she would have to live independently until a spot opened up in the high-rise. Marva's harassment of Beth continued during this period until something unexpected occurred. Marva told me that when she began having a panic attack, she took an aspirin, and the panic attack stopped. We decided that she should take an aspirin at the first hint of a panic attack. The strategy worked. Marva coped well until moving into the high-rise where she lives to this day.

Chapter 7

Health Problems and Pain Management

Health Problems

The most heart-rending aspect of a third-age counselor's job is watching health problems ravage the lives of clients. Health problems destroy or limit third-age lifestyles like no other kind of loss. Prevention is relegated to the past, for these people must deal with their bodies as they are today.

Some of your clients no doubt enjoy good health; their problems are more mental than physical. Other clients may have health problems but these problems will appear separate from their state of mind. You will also see clients whose state of mind seems to have worsened their health problems. Finally there are clients whose difficulties with anxiety or depression result almost directly from their health problems.

Chronic Health Problems and Related Stress

People with chronic illness live with diabetes, multiple sclerosis, severe arthritis, asthma, heart disease, and other medical problems. Although chronic illness is stressful in many ways, here are some of the ways that pressure is manifested:

- Pretending everything is okay

A common reaction to illness is to fight to maintain normality, but sometimes people work too hard pretending to be healthy. I know someone who has a disease of which impotency is a side effect, but this man and his wife talk about how great their sex life is. The man constantly tells off-color jokes and makes remarks about his potency. All this is a psychological defense mechanism that he uses to convince the world and himself that he is okay.

• Convincing others that you're taking necessary precautions

Diabetes is reasonably controllable, but some people have the disease to such a degree that it is brittle or uncontrollable. No matter how carefully they follow a diet and take medicine, the diabetes continues as a major problem, threatening blindness and other negative side effects. Because the public generally believes diabetes is controllable, diabetics often receive little sympathy. Even family members accuse them of not observing dietary or medicinal instructions.

• Suffering the side effects of medicine

Some medications have devastating side effects. They may cause patients to sleep most of the time, sleep poorly, or manifest psychiatric symptoms such as anxiety or depression. New diseases or new health problems sometimes result. Personality changes may also be a consequence of medication.

• Suffering inept medical attention

In a forum in the spring of 1989, Bryant Welch of the American Psychological Association remarked that "the problem of over-medication and mis-medication is so widespread that some people are calling this the nation's other drug problem." There are both highly competent and highly incompetent people in medicine. Have your clients chosen their physician with great care?

• Relationship problems

When debilitating illness strikes young, married women, their husbands often cannot cope with the situation. Many simply abandon their wives. When men are older and more mature, they usually stay. Regardless of age, many people cannot deal with the stress accompanying chronic illness, especially when their stricken partners themselves react negatively. In one situation, I know of, a husband suffered a debilitating stroke which left him so bitter that he treated his loyal wife badly, almost to the point of abuse.

• Guilt

The chronically ill inevitably must depend on others. Struck by infantile paralysis more than thirty years ago, a friend of mine is in a wheel-chair with the use of only one arm. Jeff told me that the major adjustment for him was not life in a wheelchair but his dependence on others. Some people who suffer from chronic illnesses have no choice but to ask for considerable help from others.

- Daily trials and tribulations

Living with chronic illness involves more than taking pills. Diabetics must watch their diet closely; some must take daily shots of insulin. Asthmatics live with the possibility of attacks. People with multiple sclerosis must avoid exertion, lest overtiring themselves brings on an attack. Almost every chronic illness carries with it considerations that make living difficult.

- Time-bomb chronic illness

Chronically ill people have an uncertain future. People who have had cancer never know if or when that disease will strike again. People with uncontrollable diseases live their lives in the shadow of heart disease, potential blindness, or loss of limb. People with multiple sclerosis may awaken one morning partially paralyzed. While most people with time-bomb diseases bear up well, the threats facing them are never forgotten.

- Dealing with the outside world

Often the world does not understand, does not care, or does not know how to deal with people who suffer from chronic illness. I knew a man who had been gassed in the war and could not work at a full-time job. Yet many people, seeing no visible evidence of his affliction, believed he was just lazy. Anyone around this man when he was having one of his coughing spells knew better. Illness makes people uncomfortable. Sometimes they treat victims of disease badly because they do not understand or become impatient with the person's illness.

- Increased stress

Secure people are able to deal with chronic illness. If illness places them in a wheelchair, after a period of adjustment a secure person will continue to be strong. Insecure people have difficulty dealing with all crises, minor or major. Some become depressed, and suicide is not uncommon. Asking insecure people to cope with chronic illness can sometimes exceed their capacity.

- Economic trauma

Although not all chronic illnesses result in financial problems, others create economic chaos. A family besieged by such problems may have to live with threatening letters and collection agencies. The cost of medicine alone can destroy an orderly life. A couple I know spent most of their $30,000 savings on medicine to allow the husband to live with his chronic illnesses, including Parkinson's disease, heart disease, and high blood pressure. Their monthly bill at the local pharmacy was between $200 and $300. Their savings are gone, but the couple must still pay for the medicine as well as living expenses.

- The kitchen sink

The pressures accompanying chronic illness become most apparent when people have to deal with these pressures not one at a time but simultaneously. They must deal with the disease, changes of lifestyle caused by the disease, and pressures applied by the situation. No wonder they experience depression. They can see no future only physical decline ahead.

Helping Clients with Chronic Illness

Helping clients deal with problems resulting from chronic illness may be your most difficult challenge. If the chronic illness severely changes and limits the life of the client, you can never paint a pretty picture of the future. Even if you can help your client deal with depression or anxiety, the chronic illness will always be there, so helping your client deal with depression or anxiety becomes all the more difficult.

When I work with such a client I add a couple of unique twists to conventional therapy.

Supportive Therapy

Supportive therapy is the primary mode of counseling someone with chronic illness. Sometimes an antidepressant is prescribed by the family physician along with medication for the health problem. Let your client know you are providing support—especially when the client is adjusting to the existence of the chronic health problem.

Cognitive Therapy

In small doses, cognitive therapy may sometimes be used to help a client take little steps in adapting to an illness. Often you can help your client realize that it is possible to live well despite the chronic illness. Life is not over. When cognitive therapy is used, the focus often involves developing adaptive skills and dealing with depression or anxiety.

Helping clients with health problems has always been my most difficult assignment. Often all I can do is provide support. When an agency refers a client because of depression, I know that the depression, if treated, will lift in time. But if that depression results directly from a chronic illness that offers little hope of recovery, you may face an almost impossible challenge.

Case Studies

Berta

When I visited Berta, who was referred by a local home health agency, I found a frail woman suffering from osteoporosis, anemia, and several other problems. She had to enter the hospital periodically for blood transfusions to treat her anemia, and her family physician had given her so much medication that she slept much of the day.

Despite all her health problems, Berta was faring relatively well. She and her husband Don were financially secure, and they hired enough outside help to make their lives as comfortable as possible. Don was a devoted caretaker. Although the two were coping as well as any couple could given Berta's health problems, life was difficult for them. For twenty years they had spent their winters in Florida. Due to Berta's illness, they could no longer travel. They had once socialized widely and had many friends. Their social activities were now greatly reduced in scope. Because of Berta's health problems, they now lived a very restrictive life style, leaving the house only a couple of times a week to eat at a restaurant.

I could offer little more than support. Berta's health problems would never improve. Although she suffered from depression, it was not overpowering. Her husband provided lots of support, but the case was difficult for me because I could not fix the problem. I could help other clients deal with crisis and resume their usual lifestyles. What Berta and her husband faced was not a resolvable crisis but a restricted lifestyle not subject to resolution through counseling.

Cleo

In some situations a counselor feels helpless. When Cleo was referred to me, I found a woman in her mid-eighties whose mind seemed acute but whose body had worn out. Cleo was crippled by arthritis and could not walk or feed herself. Her hands were so crippled she could not hold a fork. Basically, she could do little more than sit up with help. "I've lived too long," she told me. "I simply want to die."

When I first began seeing her, I dealt not with her spirit but with a family feud. Cleo had lived with her son Toby in their family home, a small, seven-acre farm located right in the middle of an urban area. Two months before I saw her, Cleo went into the hospital for a gall bladder operation. When Cleo returned from the hospital, she went to live with her daughter Shelly who had broken her arm and would stay home from work until the arm healed. The family agreed that when Shelly returned to work, Cleo would go elsewhere to live.

Shelly, along with two other siblings wanted Momma to enter a nursing home. Toby and Cleo wanted Momma to return home to the family farm. In typical family feud fashion, one side was not speaking to the other side. Meanwhile Cleo lay on the bed saying, "I just want to die."

I had three days to help the family solve the problem of where Cleo would live. Shelly's arm had healed and she was ready to return to work.

As an outsider, when you enter a situation, you often have considerable impact. So I engaged in some shuttle diplomacy and arranged for Momma to return to the family farm with additional services to be provided to insure that Cleo's quality of care would not fall below a minimal level. (Prior to her hospitalization, Toby reportedly had left his mother lying in bed, checking on her only a couple times a day.)

I could only provide support for Cleo when she faced serious health problems. We did an informal life review, which seemed to provide some comfort. But Cleo wanted to die, and had I been in her situation, I may have felt the same way. I could not offer Cleo reason to live, and two months after my shuttle diplomacy, she died at home in her bed. Two months after her death, Toby committed suicide.

Pain Management

On occasion you will receive a request to help a client who is dealing with chronic pain. Although the pain may be heightened by psychological perspective, it has a physical base. Some clients' pain is part of a problem rather than the main problem, but there is no doubt that third-age people suffer from more pain because of chronic health problems than do people in other age groups.

Pain in third-age people results primarily from headaches, degenerative diseases, and specific physical problems. Their headaches come not so much from migraines but from tension or muscle contraction, although headaches are often magnified in intensity because of the presence of degenerative diseases. Osteoporosis, arthritis, and other inflammatory diseases are major sources of pain. A list of diseases creating pain would include cancer, treatment of cancer, broken bones that only partly heal, and other unresolved physical problems.

Depression often accompanies chronic pain, and when an individual is lonely and bored pain is more difficult to accept. Bereavement also may increase the intensity of pain. Health also deteriorates after the death of a spouse, and chronic pain is magnified. People whose lives have become constricted, who have fewer friends and more restricted activities and interests may not have much pleasure to focus on and so make pain a point of focus.

Medication prescribed for chronic pain sometimes has negative side effects. One of my clients who suffered from advanced osteoporosis took medication that caused her to sleep fifteen hours a day. This tendency to sleep rather than to remain active made her weak. When she awakened, she experienced dizziness. Her husband had to help her walk, for he was aware of the danger of falls.

Helping Clients Suffering from Chronic Pain

Although chronic pain may have a physical cause, you can help clients who are suffering from pain in several ways:

- Encourage medical treatment

Your clients may not be doing everything possible to deal with their pain. One client whose family physician had a reputation of marginal competence refused to seek a second opinion. I finally convinced her to seek other help, and a physician at a nearby clinic prescribed a medication that immediately decreased the intensity of her pain.

- Encourage specific exercises or rehabilitation

Exercise programs designed for people with degenerative diseases increase their range of motion, strengthen muscles, increase endurance, and encourage physical activity. People who must deal with chronic pain tend to sit and avoid activity.

In most instances, a sedentary approach to dealing with pain only increases the problem. You have an obligation to find out what physical activity might benefit your client and to encourage him or her to engage in that activity.

• Provide conventional counseling

In addition to supportive therapy, attempt to increase your client's independence and level of functioning as well as to maximize feelings of self control. I have had some success using cognitive therapy, especially when in tandem with relaxation techniques. You may also have to deal with the frustration associated with chronic pain.

Case Studies

Rita

After Rita went to a hospital emergency room on three consecutive weekends complaining of chronic pain, a hospital social worker referred her to me. Rita was a sixty-eight-year-old woman, quite alert and active, who suffered from a genetic abnormality of the liver. The family physician and a consultant believed this abnormality was causing the pain. Although she was operated on to correct the abnormality, her pain continued. Again she underwent a barrage of tests, but the medical team could find no physical reason for the continuing pain.

In working with Rita I provided support to help her deal with the mild depression resulting from her physician's inability to cure her chronic pain. As a way of ruling out all causes, I encouraged her to seek a second opinion. Although the second opinion mirrored that of the first physician—neither could find a physical reason for her pain—the second physician prescribed a medication that greatly reduced the pain.

Myra

Eighty-four-year-old Myra had a hysterectomy fifty years ago and since then has had eight operations to relieve pain caused by adhesions from the hysterectomy. She would be free of pain for about five years, then the pain would reappear and increase until she required another operation.

Her current physician refused to recommend additional surgery due to her age. Myra was forced to use pain pills to lessen her pain.

To make matters worse, Myra was not a cooperative client. She was exceedingly rigid and could not relax enough to allow counseling to help. I tried relaxation exercises, and I made a tape that she played to herself at other times. Although the tape relieved the pain while she was listening to it, once she began moving around the pain returned. Myra elected to discontinue counseling and rely solely on her pain pills. Because she had been raised in an old world culture, she viewed counseling and relaxation exercises as something akin to voodoo.

Chapter 8

Marital, Relationship, and Personality Problems

Marital Problems

Marital problems do not plague recently married couples exclusively, nor are they limited to people in their late thirties or early forties who find themselves in the midst of some mid-life crisis. Although many assume that people in their sixties who have been married for twenty to forty years do not have marital problems, that belief is inaccurate. Third age couples marital difficulties usually result from one of the following situations:

- The couple had a bad marriage to begin with.

After the children leave the nest and third-age couples retire, many grow closer together. But this is not always the situation. When a couple has suffered for years in a cold and unfeeling marriage, the marriage rarely improves. In a cold marriage, one or both partners may lack the capacity to grow closer and become more supportive, or one member is forced to become a caregiver.

- Roles that allowed a couple to exist with some compatibility no longer exist.

Sometimes a marriage prevails because couples adopt somewhat bizarre compromises. For example, marriages exist in which one spouse totally dominates the other. Within the boundaries of sharply defined roles, two people may find some degree of compatibility until something happens to make these defined roles inappropriate. If a husband who has dominated a wife becomes ill, his wife, harboring years of pent-up frustration due to his treatment, may respond with indifference.

- People may not be able to endure spending twenty-four hours a day with one another.

After retirement, spouses may start spending considerably more time together than before and experience difficulties. Unused to togetherness, a couple may begin bickering. If a managerial-oriented husband begins applying his managerial skills to a household that was formerly the domain of a wife, difficulties may ensue. A good marriage is based on compromise, but some people lack the capacity to compromise.

- Age differences may catch up at retirement.

Often men marry women considerably younger, although on occasion the reverse is true. Difficult situations may result if one spouse wishes to retire fifteen years before the other. If a traditional-thinking husband retires fifteen years ahead of a working wife, he may continue to expect her to do all the housework while she continues working. She may object to such an allocation of responsibilities.

- One spouse cannot accept the role of caregiver.

Not every person enters the third age with a capacity to be an effective caregiver. When sickness of a spouse or an adult child forces a person into a caregiving role, he or she may be unable to fill such a role. The caregiving role may cause stress on the relationship. If the relationship was weak to begin with, this new source of stress can destroy it.

- Problems within a family may create difficulties between spouses.

In a society in which the melded family is fast becoming the norm, a potential for divisiveness exists. If a melded family consists of two children from each remarried spouse, and if one of the adult children has difficulty coping with life, an aging parent who requires lots of care from his or her spouse may be undermined.

- Disagreements over lifestyles may occur.

Sometimes disagreements occur over what kind of lifestyle a couple may choose. One spouse may want to maintain a family home while another spouse may want to move; or one may want to spend winters in a different state while another does not; or one spouse may want to stay home most of the time while the other may want to socialize. Sometimes a couple may compromise or reach agreements over issues. Other times a couple may spend the rest of their lives in a smoldering feud.

Therapy for Marital Problems

Most third-age clients who opt for help with their marriage do not want extensive counseling. I use a four-session plan. In the first session, I see the couple together to get a feeling for what the issues are and how the partners relate to one another. Frequently I find that the wife wants to make changes in the relationship while the husband maintains that their marriage is okay as it is.

In the second and third sessions, I see the husband and wife individually. In these sessions I urge each person to ventilate and describe the situation from his or her point of view. Then I list and seek agreement of the person on the major concern, the perspective of each spouse, the strengths of the marriage, the areas in which they agree, and how each might compromise. Before each session ends, I like to have total agreement that the perspective I present is accurate from the point of view of each spouse.

The fourth and final session is the most important. Rarely is the problem one-sided. (When one spouse is to blame for the situation, that person usually refuses marital counseling.) But often the situation may be seventy-thirty rather than fifty-fifty. When it is a seventy-thirty situation, I attempt to make it appear to be fifty-fifty. The role of the counselor, or mediator, can be effective only if both man and wife believe the counselor or mediator is fair.

Prior to this final session, I prepare a one-page summary and recommendation using this format:

The Problem: _____

The Husband's Perspective: _____

The Wife's Perspective: _____

Mutual Agreement and Strengths: _____

Possible Compromises: _____

Without handing out copies, I go over each aspect in detail, encouraging the participants to correct me if my perspective is inaccurate in any way. After both husband and wife are satisfied, I give each a copy of my outline. The degree of success they achieve depends upon the effort the husband and wife are willing to make.

When in resolving their conflicts you encounter a couple with marital problems, conflict resolution is usually the best approach to use. This approach will work so long as both husband and wife are willing to bend a bit. If one or the other refuses to engage in rational compromise, you may not be able to help.

Case Studies

Ray and Helen

Helen was eight years older than Ray and they had married twenty years ago, when Helen was fifty-two and Ray was forty-four. Ray had been divorced; Helen had no prior marriage. They were different in other ways, too. Helen was very organized, very methodical, an always-do-the-right-thing person, while Ray was a bit of a free spirit, a man who cared little for money and insisted on following his desires.

Now they were at the point of divorce. Helen wanted a normal retirement; Ray was still interested in his career. Helen had saved her money during her career years and frugally watched every penny; Ray had a tendency to become involved in get-rich-quick schemes, even though he cared little about money. Helen resented Ray's outside activities that kept him busy much of the time. As a result of these activities, Helen was angry and ready to pounce on Ray at the slightest provocation. Ray simply withdrew, ignored her, and did his own thing.

When Helen asked me to intervene to save the marriage, I suspected that she wanted me to support her and criticize Ray. Because he expected that same treatment—I had known Helen earlier, having seen her a few times the previous year—Ray at first seemed distant. Usually, the most difficult aspect of marital counseling is convincing both parties that you will be fair to all involved, but this was not difficult with Ray and Helen, for both were at fault. Helen was too demanding; Ray was too intent on following personal goals.

In counseling Ray and Helen, I used the one-page summary and recommendation sheet.

The Problem

Helen and Ray are different people. Helen is a conservative thinking, ready-to-sit-and-rock woman who is tired of free-spirited Ray doing his own thing. They have totally different perspectives on life and their time together.

Helen's Perspective

Ray is a self-absorbed free spirit more interested in his clubs and his marginally successful business interests than he is in her.

Ray's Perspective

Helen is a domineering woman who wants him to conform to her rules and pounces on him for no reason.

Mutual Agreement

Both have health problems. Both want the marriage to survive. Both admit that if the marriage is to survive each had to make some compromises.

Possible Compromises

Helen agrees to stop trying to dominate Ray. A free spirit, he will continue to withdraw and become even more self-absorbed if she continues her attempt to change him. Ray must remember that, in a marriage, each partner must consider the other person. He will reduce his level of self absorption.

This approach worked with Helen and Ray, for both were willing to compromise to save their marriage. The two had spent the last few years involved in a power struggle, with each trying to coerce the other into living his or her lifestyle. Once they realized that some relatively minor compromises could result in a better marriage, both agreed. All Ray had to do every month or so was to schedule enough time for a short trip with Helen. All Helen had to do was to recognize Ray's right to live his life—or rather his life with some adjustments—as he desired.

Art and Susanna

Art and Susanna had been married for forty years. They now were sixty-two and fifty-eight, respectively. They had been relatively happy, but for the last couple of years Art had become disenchanted with their marriage. Art was a conventional man. He spent most of his adult years working as an insurance broker, but retired a few months earlier on his sixty-second birthday.

Susanna was decidedly unconventional. Although she would soon be fifty-nine, she continued to dress and act as if she were twenty-five. She worked hard at retaining her figure. She kept her hair long and dyed black. Until recently her attempt at retaining her youthful appearance lent her a flattering appearance. As she approached her sixties, however, her faux youthfulness was garish.

The major problem between the two was not Susanna's attempt to maintain her youth and her flirtatious ways, but her attitude toward their son Sammy, their only child. Susanna focused her life on keeping her son dependent upon her. Although Sammy was in his mid-thirties, he continued living with his parents. Sammy and his mother often did things together, going shopping and to the movies. He had no life other than his life with his mother.

It was Art who called in asking for help. "I don't believe I can take this much longer," Art said. "She doesn't include me in her life at all. And she has turned our son into some sort of sissy."

I began a very difficult martial counseling. Art was obviously correct and Susanna was in the wrong, but Susanna saw nothing wrong in her relationship with her son.

Susanna agreed to three sessions. When they came in, I saw each of them for thirty minutes and then met with them together for a few minutes. In the first thirty minutes, I realized that the most difficult aspect of the problem was convincing Susanna that her relationship with her son was harming him and destroying her marriage. I had no success doing this. I convinced Susanna to see another counselor for one session, but this other therapist was also unsuccessful. Art continues to attempt to decide if he wants to stay in the marriage. When he raises the issue, Susanna doesn't seem to care. She says she and her son will survive without Art.

Change can come about only when people are motivated to change. Susanna was not motivated because the suggested change offered her nothing. She did not believe she was harming her son. She did not care if Art disliked the situation. If Art wanted to end the marriage, Susanna felt that it was his privilege.

Relationship Problems

You will encounter clients whose relationship difficulties contribute to or are the major source of a problem. It is especially difficult to deal with relationships when treating several people, all of whom have difficulty coping with life. Many relationship problems stem from one person, with that person having forced others into skewed roles.

Relationship difficulties can be divided into two general categories:

1. Relationship problems the counselor cannot resolve

A counselor can help only people who want to be helped. I once worked with a client named Vivian whose major difficulty revolved around her daughter Jana—Vivian's only relative—who treated her quite shabbily. Although I made considerable progress with Vivian, I never could help her to the degree I wanted, for she continued to fuel her depression with plaintive wails about how Jana did not love her. I saw Jana in three counseling sessions, but she had no interest in her mother. She was only interested in how she might cement a tentative relationship with her third husband, from whom she was divorced.

2. Relationship problems the counselor can resolve

Not all relationship difficulties are unresolvable, of course. When people want to improve a relationship, you can make great progress by pointing out major sources of problems and then negotiating changes. Bear in mind that participants must have the capacity to modify behavior before you can negotiate change.

Helping Clients with Relationship Difficulties

When dealing with a client who has relationship difficulties with someone who will not move or cooperate, I attempt to help my client live more independently. I use this approach because there is usually no other choice. In the case involving Vivian and Jana, I helped Vivian deal with her depression and create a life for herself that was not so dependent on her daughter. With a client and an individual or family with the capacity to correct their relationship, I like to use conflict resolution, an approach based on the book *From Conflict to Resolution* by Susan Heitler.

In her perception of conflict resolution, Heitler maintains there are three general components to resolving conflicts:

1. The process is based on talking, not on verbal or physical violence or bullying.

2. The process is primarily cooperative. People work together rather than attempt to coerce one another.

3. The participants agree to an outcome or settlement that addresses the concerns of all and is acceptable to all participants.

Use conflict resolution when the participants willingly desire to pursue a mutual agreement. This approach fails when one participant enters the process determined to emerge the winner. In some situations, marital counseling in particular, it is possible to convince a recalcitrant participant to engage in legitimate conflict resolution. Emily so hounded her daughter Evelyn with telephone calls that Evelyn left her telephone off the hook much of the day. This upset Emily so much that she refused to engage in any sort of mediation. When I subtly explained to Emily that if she did not negotiate a satisfactory arrangement Evelyn was going to move out of town, she relented. We arrived at some ground rules for the telephone, and everyone was happy. Everyone won.

Conflict resolution is a theory of negotiation conceived in the late 1950s and early 1960s. It involves:

- Clarification of issues
- Assistance to help each side understand the position of the other participants
- Calming of hostile attitudes.
- Introduction of a third party—the counselor—to act as mediator
- Dividing the major issue into more manageable units
- Identifying the goals of all parties
- Establishing a general way of dealing with situations before something happens to create a crisis.
- Encouragement to look at the total picture and devise a solution that seems acceptable to all

When conflict resolution is used, negotiation consists of three major phases:

1. Expression of initial positions

In this phase, each side expresses their initial positions. With the mother and daughter who were in conflict over the mother's telephone calls, the mother felt quite insecure and had adapted the child's role in the relationship. She was lonely and wanted to talk to her daughter several times a day, although she really had nothing to say. The daughter, who cringed each time the telephone rang, felt the mother was disrupting her life by calling so often.

2. Discussion of underlying concerns

A concern is a feeling or belief about one's self or one's world. Emily, the mother in the telephone situation, was a very insecure woman who loved her daughter Evelyn very much. Yet Emily knew Evelyn was drifting away. In her insecure perspective, Emily attempted to solidify the relationship by calling Evelyn more often, asking to spend more time together. Evelyn was concerned about Emily and felt a normal obligation to help her elderly mother, but felt she could not deal with the calls, which were indeed a form of harassment.

3. Acceptance of a solution by all participants

A solution is a course of action, a way of meeting participants' underlying concerns. Acting as mediator between mother and daughter, I helped Emily and Evelyn arrive at a mutually satisfying solution. They agreed it was all right for Emily to call her once a day. Evelyn agreed to this solution, for she wanted to make contact with her mother at least once a day to make certain Emily was all right. Although she would have preferred calling several times a day, Emily found that by limiting calls to once a day Evelyn was more responsive to her.

Case Studies

The Butzs

Luke and Ida Butz had been married fifty-two years when I began seeing them. During those fifty-two years, Luke spent more time with "the boys," than with Ida who remained in the home as the homemaker. Luke had worked at a factory during the day, played golf in the spring and summer, and bowled in the winter. He often met the boys at the tavern or coffee shop after work and on weekends. When Luke and Ida were together in the evening, Luke totally dominated the relationship. He did what he wanted and Ida acceded to his wishes without question. Their life changed little after Luke retired. Luke simply spent more time with the boys. Then disaster disrupted their lives. Ida had a stroke, and Luke had to stay home and care for her.

Luke subsequently became depressed—not so much because of what had happened to Ida, but because her illness had disrupted his lifestyle.

Given such a situation, I could make only peripheral changes. I arranged for Luke to receive a mild antidepressant and some respite care. But he and his wife had spent a lifetime developing their rather bizarre relationship, and neither appeared capable of change or even wanted change.

Harriet

Harriet called the crisis center one morning, and after listening to her problem, the crisis center called me. I visited Harriet that afternoon, and met a nervous, seventy-seven year-old woman with an old-world accent who lived in a nice house decorated in 1930s style. Harriet had undergone a hysterectomy three months earlier. She was to begin radiation treatment the next week. A widow for a dozen years, Harriet was in otherwise good health. She lived an active life and thought young. "Seventy-seven is not old," she said, and she believed it.

Her problem was her daughter, who would arrive from Boston in two days. From previous conversations, Harriet knew that when Sonja came, she would attempt to persuade Harriet to sell her house and move into a small apartment in Boston. "I don't want to leave my house and my things," Harriet said. "I'm not old yet."

I first reassured Harriet that she had rights: she did not have to accede to her daughter's wishes. Obviously, Harriet had not reached the point where she could no longer care for herself; and until or unless she reached that point, she did not have to submit to Sonja's pressure. I offered to talk with Sonja when she arrived from Boston.

Two days later, Harriet called and what followed perfectly illustrates conflict resolution.

Here were the initial positions: Sonja wanted Harriet to move to Boston so that she could watch over her aging mother. Harriet did not want to leave her house, her things, her friends, and move to a large city where she knew no one.

Underlying concerns: Sonja feared her mother had reached the point in life where she could no longer care for herself adequately, especially after a hysterectomy and radiation treatments. Harriet believed the time when she could no longer care for herself was still years away.

Solution: After going through the negotiating process, I helped Harriet and Sonja agree that Harriet would remain in her house as long as she was able to care for herself. When or if Harriet reached the stage where she might have difficulty remaining independent, she would consider moving to Boston.

I have checked on Harriet periodically since then, but she has never required counseling. These two sessions sufficed.

Personality Problems

People with "personality problems" cannot exist compatibly with other people. Although there are many such problems, clients who are belligerent pose particular difficulty for counselors and their agencies. Belligerence does not describe all personality problems, but hostile, aggressive clients are among the most difficult people to work with.

Difficulties in life, stressful relationships, and personality disorders are just a few of the situations that create belligerency. Often a combination of situations coalesce in belligerency.

Unfortunately, bringing about major changes in third-age clients with personality problems is almost impossible. Belligerent people have spent a lifetime becoming what they are, and being belligerent is their normal state. People *can* change, but belligerent people often find no reason to change. They believe that the rest of the world is at fault and that they are correct in all things.

Change occurs only when belligerent clients believes it is in their best interest to modify their behavior. Although a belligerent person's essential style rarely changes, such a person can sometimes modify behavior and attitude. The potential for change increases greatly when a belligerent client is threatened with the cessation of essential services. I was once asked to intervene in a unique situation in which a ninety-seven-year-old man was denied eating privileges at a local senior center because he refused to bathe and treated the servers with disrespect. I saw Ryan for thirty minutes one time only and informed him he was to bathe weekly and stop complaining about the food or lose his privilege permanently. Because eating at the senior center was important to him, Ryan began bathing and remained quiet when he went through the serving line. In short, belligerent people will change only when there is a reward or the fear of loss. Belligerency for these people is normal; treating others with respect is abnormal.

Case Studies

Tom

Tom was referred to the center when he was discharged after a hospital stay. He could not otherwise get the services that he needed to continue to live independently. Although he was only sixty-five, he had been a lifetime heavy smoker, had serious pulmonary problems, and required oxygen. Housekeepers came twice weekly to help him clean. Some were black, and Tom was strongly biased against black people. He had frightened one housekeeper with a baseball bat and B-B gun. As a result, the housekeeper refused to serve Tom, and the agency that provided the help decided it could not assist him.

When I began working with Tom, I knew that I could not counsel him out of his racial biases, so I attempted to bargain him into accepting services. Because Tom could barely walk, we both knew he needed services, but the agency would not restore services without some concessions. With Tom's permission, I mediated with the agency, which agreed to restore services if Tom would promise to get rid of his B-B gun and accept black housekeepers without subjecting them to his racial slurs. Although Tom did not want to make these concessions, he realized he had no choice. The agreement was made and adhered to. Tom was still racist, but he was able to modify his behavior when it was vital to his self interest to do so.

Mary Ruth

I received a call from the manager of a local high-rise who had pressured a resident into agreeing to seek counseling. Mary Ruth had already been evicted from one high-rise, and she was on the verge of being evicted from another. She simply could not get along with other residents. Working with Mary Ruth proved quite an experience. Because she did not want to be seen coming into the mental health center and did not want me to visit her at the high-rise, we met at a local church for our first session.

Before she said one word to me, I witnessed the unpleasantness that was part and parcel of Mary Ruth's life. As she passed the church secretary's desk, she stopped and without provocation berated the secretary for a perceived slight. During the first five minutes of our first session, she berated me three times for perceived slights. Then, in the next half hour, I learned that Mary Ruth had undergone three divorces in the first ten years of her adult life—this in an era when divorce was socially unacceptable.

I couldn't work with Mary Ruth. She believed that she was correct and the rest of the world had conspired to make life difficult for her. I babied her through two sessions. She quit after the third session when I had the audacity to suggest that she modify her approach. She disagreed. Mary Ruth believed the world should adapt to her.

Chapter 9

Lifestyle Dissatisfaction, Lifelong Problems, and Substance Abuse

Lifestyle Dissatisfaction

Characteristics of third-age clients suffering from lifestyle dissatisfaction often include the following:

- Dissatisfaction with life prior to entering the third age

Life for the dissatisfied has been flat almost from the beginning. They lack zest for life. To expect them to find delight in the third age is unrealistic. After exploring the backgrounds of these clients, I find almost without fail a mildly dysfunctional life—an alcoholic father or spouse, and a divorce or two. Whatever the cause, these clients have not lived a life in which they found fulfillment.

- Conflict in life

People who are dissatisfied with their lives have difficulty with friends or family. Expect to find feuds with relatives or friends. You'll hear statement like, "I haven't spoken to my son for more than five years. His wife won't allow it." Or: "My brother just stopped coming around a few years ago. I don't know why." Rarely has anyone made any attempt to deal with whatever problems underlie the conflict.

- Failure to adapt and adjust to changes in life

Change accompanies the third age, especially the frail years, and demands adjustment and adaptation. People must adjust to living on a smaller income, giving up a car, and making other significant changes. Dissatisfied people continue to express dissatisfaction for what has happened to change their lives. Often, they talk of their disenchantment repeatedly and to whomever will listen.

Helping Clients who are Dissatisfied with Life

Clients who are dissatisfied with life offer counselors a major challenge. There are several reasons why this kind of person is difficult to deal with. They have often spent a lifetime getting to the point where they are ready to ask for assistance. Helping the client deal with this backlog of unhappiness in a relatively short time creates huge demands on both the counselor and the client. The client who is dissatisfied with life usually filters life through a negative mindset that creates barriers to detract from every suggestion you might offer. Many dissatisfied people have viewed the world through negative mindsets for so long, they may not really believe that they can change and live a more contented life.

Armed with the knowledge that dealing with a dissatisfied person has serious built-in difficulties, how might you work with such a client?

1. Provide support.

Although providing support is important with all clients, it is particularly important with these clients. Dissatisfied clients are distrustful of people in general; they are always looking for excuses to criticize individuals and classes of people. Build support not only through conventional counseling, but also by concrete actions. Doing special little things will help develop trust.

2. Deal with the dissatisfied client in much the same way that you deal with a person suffering from depression.

Because depression often accompanies dissatisfaction with life, adopting techniques for treating depression seems effective, especially cognitive techniques for appropriate clients. Set attainable goals, break large tasks into small ones, set priorities, and encourage your client to participate in activities that provide enjoyment. Exercise also helps.

3. Work at changing the client's mindset.

Clients with a distorted view of the world, probably will not find relief. Working on changing a person's mindset therefore becomes important. A person suffering from depression may have become depressed as the result of a specific event; whereas, the dissatisfied person often has spent a lifetime feeling left out.

4. Work on situations that may have created a lifetime of dissatisfaction.

People are not born dissatisfied with life; things happen to them that create dissatisfaction. No matter the cause, dissatisfied clients will view everything thereafter as being negative. Exploring and analyzing the causes of dissatisfaction with your client may provide him or her with a more rational perspective on life.

However, don't expect too much. You can make only as much progress as your client will allow. If your client continues to insist upon a distorted view of life, only token progress is usually possible.

Case Studies

Maud

Maud lived in a housing complex on less than $500 a month. She paid $82 a month rent, but her apartment was comfortable and immaculately clean. The rest of her life was not as orderly, for she was in almost constant conflict with everyone—not major knock-down, drag-out conflict, but no matter what anyone did, Maud reacted with hostility.

I once drove Maud to her optometrist to have her eyeglasses adjusted. When she saw the receptionist, rather than explaining that her eyeglasses needed to be adjusted, she adopted a confrontational attitude and glared at the receptionist. "I got these glasses here three weeks ago and I can't wear them because they hurt my nose!" she accused. And this was the way Maud lived her life. When doing her family history, I found that although she had been married almost fifty years, she had lived with her husband for only five years. Although Maud had two children, she had not spoken to her son for five years and she had a tenuous relationship with her daughter.

After my first session with Maud, I suspected that she was someone with whom I could make only minimal progress. Subsequent visits substantiated that belief. Although she was always pleasant with me, she viewed every encounter with the world as an altercation.

I worked with Maud for fourteen sessions, providing emotional and physical support as well as transportation. I had hoped to arrange for an antidepressant to help her deal with her dysthymia, a form of depression, but Maud refused. "I can't afford it," she said. I suggested ways she might better deal with the world, but I don't know that she took any of my suggestions. I do know that she coped better with life during the period in which I worked with her.

Georgia

Georgia was seventy-nine and lived in a high-rise. The first time I visited her, she immediately began complaining about life there. She had lived most of her life on a farm, and she missed it. She was used to living a more solitary life and she disliked having so many people around her, although she socialized very little with other residents. Georgia had a lengthy list of complaints, and it seemed that nothing about her life was positive.

Georgia had one legitimate complaint. After a late-in-life divorce, she'd married Luke, a farmer, but in the twenty years she was married to him, her relationship with Luke's two children and his family was never very good. Then five years ago her husband had displayed the first symptoms of Alzheimer's disease.

She cared for him at home as long as she could, but then she had to place him in a nursing home. It was a legitimate placement; she had reached the point where she could no longer care for Luke.

Her husband's two sons lived in Arizona and apparently cared little for their father. Still they and Luke's sister complained constantly to Georgia about her inability to keep her husband at home. The sons apparently were concerned only about their inheritance being decimated by the cost of nursing home care, while the sister had unreal expectations of what Georgia could do for him. Eventually, nursing home care ate up all the money, and Luke was forced to accept Medicaid assistance for his nursing home care. The family continued to blame Georgia, who had handled the situation properly, as far as I could ascertain. Georgia had no other choice, but Luke's relatives caused her great distress.

When I began working with Georgia, I learned that other counselors had worked with her on the same problem. After checking her files, I discovered a pattern: Georgia would come in asking for help, see a counselor two or three times to deal with the immediate crisis involving her in-laws, and then discontinue the sessions. Knowing this, I suggested that we compose a letter that I would mail from the mental health center to her in-laws. In this letter, subject to Georgia's approval, I would state that Georgia's problems were directly related to the stress placed upon her by her in-laws. I would then follow up this letter with a telephone call, emphasizing the points addressed in the letter. I knew that although this tactic might relieve much of Georgia's unhappiness, her dissatisfaction with life would continue.

When I first approached Georgia with this suggestion, she was ecstatic. She believed that my writing the letter and making the telephone call might relieve the pressure she was under. Several times I had said to her, "Georgia, you have absolutely nothing to lose. To make these people stop harassing you, we must emphasize that what they are doing is endangering your health." It was an accurate statement because the pressure of the monthly visit and harassment by her husband's sister placed great stress on her.

We decided that I would return in three days, at which time we would jointly compose the letter. But when I returned and knocked on Georgia's door in the high-rise, I received no answer; Georgia was not home. When I reached her by telephone a few days later, she said she had decided against the approach; she would deal with the situation by herself.

It was typical of Georgia's philosophy of life. When something happened, she simply withdrew. Perhaps she was unwilling to change her indirect way of dealing with problems.

Lifelong Problems

Ninety percent of the time third-age counseling involves working with people who are in crisis or having difficulty making transitions. On occasion, you will encounter a client who has had a lifetime of problems.

I am not referring here to individuals who have suffered from schizophrenia or manic depression, because these individuals have likely had a lifetime of care from other agencies. In our mental health center, a group of case managers watch over these individuals, making certain they have medication and a place to live. The clients I refer to as having lifetime problems have successfully lived independently all their lives.

The 10 percent who fit into the category of having lifetime problems generally exhibit four characteristics:

1. They come from dysfunctional families.

When I record the family history of clients with lifetime problems, invariably their family history includes multiple marriages, poor health habits resulting in premature deaths, instances of alcohol or drug abuse, and considerable discord among family members. Often, emotional and physical abuse has also occurred.

2. Most have been in counseling early in life or on an occasional basis.

Both individuals described below had periods in their lives in which they had undergone extensive counseling. Both had enjoyed extended periods of stability; however, when crises occurred, both required help. Because of previous positive counseling experiences, these individuals will seek help in a crisis rather than tough it out the way many people do.

3. Most live a tenuous life.

People with lifetime problems lack reserves to draw upon when under stress. Something happens that would have little effect on someone with normal emotional reserves but is beyond the capacity of a person with lifetime problems to deal with. It's as if anxiety or depression is ready to surface at the slightest provocation.

4. They are basically unhappy.

Even those clients with supportive families seem to be unhappy people. They often live with the burden of earlier negative experiences in life, and these experiences seem to dominate their lives to the extent that they cannot enjoy the little things in life.

Helping Clients with Lifetime Problems

Because their problems vary so much, it is difficult to make specific suggestions for helping people with lifetime problems, but two approaches are generally appropriate:

• Help your client relieve the symptoms.

Whatever the symptoms, help relieve them. Sometimes these symptoms are anxiety or depression. Your client may need help with a crisis, or mediation in a dispute with relatives. The problem may involve a combination of symptoms—depression resulting from a crisis with a relative, anxiety over a health problem, or other situations that have produced frustration.

• Work with your client on lifetime problems.

Clients with lifetime problems may not understand the crux of their situation, but most can identify the essential problem. Your client may refuse to deal with the underlying problem responsible for the current crisis, but if he or she does opt to work on the lifetime problem, it will take numerous counseling sessions. After all, the problem has probably burdened your client for half a century or more.

Case Studies

Carol

Carol called and straightway said, "I felt it was about time I got some counseling." When I met her, I found an attractive, very pleasant, seemingly together person. On first impression, I wondered if she really required help. By the second session, I realized that Carol came from a dysfunctional family, had been married three times, and had periodically been very promiscuous.

The state had once taken away her children and she had been in and out of counseling for thirty-five years. Despite a life of living on the edge, Carol managed to reach her sixth decade of life with a measure of stability. I primarily provided her with support. In the four months that we worked together, we moved from crisis to crisis.

First it was her mother, who it seemed had made her a fragile person. Next it was her job with which she was having trouble coping. Rather than having an occasional major crisis, Carol experienced a series of minor crises.

Almost any concern seemed more than she could comfortably handle, but eventually Carol reached a point where she could deal with most of her problems. She continues to call me with her major concerns.

Annette

Sixty-six-year-old Annette lived by herself in a studio apartment. She walked a lot, and one day while she was crossing a busy street in front of her apartment, she was hit by a car and broke her leg. Because she had not dealt well with being restricted to her apartment for two months, she was referred to me by another agency. Unlike many third-age clients, Annette was a client who would have benefited from two-year, twice-weekly analysis.

Born into a family quite high on the social scale, she had spent her early years amid many luxuries. But Annette's mother was a basically cold, Victorian, self-centered woman whose two children were cared for by servants. Annette's father, a successful businessman, spent most of his life in the business world. While this preoccupation with business fits the mold for many men of that era, I got the impression that he worked long hours in part to escape the company of his wife.

Annette was twenty-eight when her mother died and she learned that she and her brother had been what she called 'foster children.' "I was probably illegitimate," Annette said. She became obsessed with her heritage. It haunted her so much that she consulted several psychiatrists and had spent several months as a resident in a mental institution. Along the way she married and divorced. She had a negative relationship with her daughter, from whom she had been estranged for fifteen years.

Although I had no illusions about solving all of Annette's ingrained problems, I wanted to help her. I began by explaining that her parents' action in not telling their children of their heritage, was very much in keeping with the thinking of the day. We had just begun working with her extreme anger when Annette discontinued the sessions.

Annette had worked with many psychiatrists over the years, but none had seemed to help her. I suspected that it was not the psychiatrists who were at fault. Annette was unable to confront the long-held and disturbing feelings about her family situation. She believed that these feelings were too painful to face.

I hope that one day Annette will call and resume counseling.

Substance Abuse

Alcoholism as it relates to third-age people has largely been ignored. Most programs for alcoholism and substance abuse have been set up for other age groups. In part this is understandable. Most long-term alcoholics die before receiving their first Social Security check. However, some alcoholics do survive into their third age. Moreover, several studies have found that one third of third-age alcoholics became alcoholics after entering their third age. This syndrome is described as late onset alcoholism. Other studies have found that only 15 percent of this group receive treatment. Perhaps most frightening, the percentage of third-age people suffering from alcoholism appears to be increasing.

The problem of alcoholism increases for third-age people because a person's tolerance for alcohol decreases with age. A person can become intoxicated on a smaller quantity of alcohol and remain affected for a longer period of time. Because third-age people take considerable medication for health problems, there is a possibility of medication and alcohol acting in combination, resulting in an adverse reaction. With all this as backdrop, two questions are relevant:

1. Why do some people begin drinking after receiving their first Social Security check?

The pressures involved in living as a third-age person include boredom; a perceived loss of status, power, and authority; marital problems; loss of a spouse; health problems; loneliness and isolation. Third-age alcoholics rarely fit the image of skid row alcoholics, who almost always die earlier in life. Often, a third-age alcoholic is someone who might have been drinking slightly to excess prior to retirement, and then after retirement begins drinking considerably more. For some individuals, drinking to excess is a new experience. While some people cope well with the pressures of the third age, others have difficulty dealing with pressures and look for other ways to cope. Some cope by becoming problem drinkers.

2. How can you detect third-age alcoholism?

People with a history of excessive drinking who survive into their third age, rarely change their lifestyle. Family and friends know they have been drinking to excess much of their life and do not expect them to change. Those who become alcoholics after reaching their third age remain part of a hidden population. Not only do they feel ashamed and attempt to hide their excessive drinking, but their families also become ashamed of their behavior. Family members participate in a kind of conspiracy to keep that person part of the hidden population. Women in particular often hide their drinking, and the problem is all the more difficult to detect. Not long ago I was speaking with a third-age person who related a story about his sister's hidden alcoholism. He had discovered that his sister, who lives alone in another city, had just entered treatment for alcoholism. The family had no hint that the woman had been drinking to excess for ten years.

Recent third-age problem drinkers exhibit these symptoms:

- Short-term memory loss
- Loss of appetite

- Mood swings—alternating crying or becoming hostile
- Untidiness in personal appearance or maintaining an unclean home
- Medication does not seem to work as effectively or in the same way
- Appearance of cuts, bruises from falls, or repeated falling
- If the person smokes, burns may appear from carelessness with cigarettes
- General loss of interest in family activities and hobbies

Although alcoholism peaks between ages of thirty-five and fifty and then declines with increasing age, a second peak occurs between ages sixty-five to seventy-four. The highest rate of alcoholism in men is found in widowers; the highest rate of alcoholism in women is found among women sixty and above. One study found that of third-age people admitted to psychiatric wards in hospitals, a fourth of these people were heavily involved with alcohol. In another study in which those sixty-plus were charged with minor crimes, 82 percent suffered from alcoholism. Another study found that the three major problems leading to alcohol abuse of third-age people were difficulty adjusting to a retirement lifestyle, an increased awareness of death, and loneliness.

Helping Third-Age Alcoholics

You will probably not see many alcoholics as clients, because most remain hidden or reach such a depth of despair that they go directly into treatment programs. Even so, you have two obligations:

1. Remember to remind others that excessive use of alcohol is a common problem among third-age people.

2. Discuss the problem of third-age alcoholism with healthcare professionals. Even when the problem is recognized and diagnosed, professionals often make no referral because they feel hopeless about treating older alcoholics. However, older alcoholics, and especially late onset alcoholics, can be helped if they participate in effective treatment programs. Healthcare professionals and counselors need to break the cycle of shame and denial that prevents third-age alcoholics from getting help.

If you suspect alcoholism in your client, there are ten questions that can help you substantiate whether a problem exists:

1. Has your client's personality or behavior changed recently?
2. Has your client appeared confused or suffered memory loss?
3. Has your client become more socially isolated and remained at home much of the time?
4. Has your client become more argumentative?
5. Has your client been neglecting personal hygiene, eating irregularly, or missing appointments?
6. Has your client had difficulty managing his or her affairs?
7. Has your client been neglecting medical treatment?
8. Has your client had difficulties with the law?
9. Has your client had difficulties with neighbors?
10. Has drinking been associated with any of the other difficulties?

When you review these questions, note also that some of the same questions might be asked of your clients suspected of depression or dementia. Similarities exist among sufferers of alcoholism, depression, and dementia.

Arranging Treatment for Third-Age Alcoholics

After detecting alcoholism in a client, treating substance abuse involves two approaches that might be used. These approaches might also be used with a long-term alcoholic who because of a strong body has survived into the third age, although the likelihood of a cure remains bleak. If the alcoholism is merely a symptom of other problems—in the same way that depression or anxiety is usually little more than a symptom—then you might try to work with the client's underlying problems. If your client has the resolve to deal with the problem, you might achieve some success. You might diagnose depression and overlook your client's alcoholism, but this approach will succeed only if your client is already determined to deal with the difficulty. Although older drinkers often resist referral into structured treatment programs, they are reasonably effective. The program involves detoxification, a hospital stay, outpatient services, and an after-care support group. Your major difficulty will be in finding a treatment program that is affordable and that deals primarily with third-age clients. A support group in which most of the individuals are in their thirties but includes one person of seventy-two creates a disadvantage for the older alcoholic who simply does not mesh well with people having different pressures and concerns. Unfortunately, most programs aimed specifically at older alcoholics are private and expensive. And yet, older alcoholics, especially those with late onset alcoholism, are not beyond help if they enter treatment programs.

Case Studies

David

David enjoyed a very successful career in industry traveling all over the world. China became a second home to him. He was used to a high-profile life, troubleshooting problems, traveling in limousines, before returning home to the office and his wife.

Then a British firm bought the corporation, and at age fifty-eight, David was forced to retire. Although he said he enjoyed retirement, David began drinking a little more each month until his wife Ursula recognized the developing problem.

I talked with David for thirty minutes and then with his wife for another thirty minutes. They were smart, perceptive people. David did not believe that he had a problem, but he understood his wife's concern. "I will quit drinking," he said, deciding to deal with the problem in this way, but both he and his wife realized that the probable reason for his drinking was that he had nothing to do. He had gone from a high-pressure job to total idleness. Neither David nor Ursula were surprised or disagreed when I suggested that David needed to find something to do. Since finances were not a problem, volunteering was the obvious approach. I made several suggestions and scheduled an appointment to see him in three weeks. When I returned three weeks later, I learned that David had checked into several possibilities and settled on a part-time position teaching mathematics to high school students who needed special instruction. The next time I saw David, he had begun teaching, was enthralled with the job, and spoke enthusiastically for an hour about his new focus in life.

David dealt with the problem himself. I had simply given him some common sense advice.

Melany

I was called by hospital discharge planners and asked to help Melany. A very attractive eighty-eight-year-old woman, Melany was brought into the hospital with a broken hip but soon began exhibiting withdrawal symptoms. It became obvious to the hospital that Melany was an alcoholic.

She lived with her second husband, John, who was two years younger than she but who walked in a bent-over style because of osteoporosis. John and Melany had married when they were seventy, both after losing their spouses. They had lots of money and lived an upper-class lifestyle. A striking couple, they traveled a lot and spent their winters in a condominium in Naples, Florida.

Tests revealed that Melany's organs were still in relatively good condition, indicating that she had become an alcoholic only in the last few years. Apparently their normal drinking style of a couple of cocktails a day had changed, and Melany was now drinking steadily. John became the enabler—buying the liquor and drinking with Melany.

Melany continually referred to "how horrible I look." I suspected that Melany, still a strikingly attractive woman, began drinking after she had perceived that her looks were deteriorating. Blessed by fate with beauty, she had probably used her looks as a crutch all her life. When she felt her beauty was disappearing, she began to drink.

Working with her husband, we arranged for Melany to enter a private treatment program for detoxification. This was a very expensive program. It followed conventional alcoholism treatment programs, but because it was restricted to older clients, a greater emphasis was given to clients' medical condition. After four weeks, Melany was placed in a nursing home—she simply could not care for herself. Although he could have lived independently for awhile, John elected to go with her. Economics was not a consideration, so they chose an exceptionally good nursing home over in-home services.

Chapter 10

Dementia and Late Onset Paranoia

Dementia

Nothing associated with the third age frightens people more than the possibility of dementia. Many people believe they can deal with the losses, illnesses, and other problems of the frail years, but not with dementia. Only a small percentage of third-age people suffer from dementia, and yet the percentage increases with age. At least one in five individuals eighty-five and older have some degree of dementia. More often, it is the fear of dementia that poses a significant problem. Sometimes individuals, families, or friends diagnose memory problems as Alzheimer's disease and become depressed or anxious.

Symptoms of Dementia

Early symptoms of dementia are sometimes so slight they pass unnoticed. Some sufferers may successfully mask their symptoms for months, even years in cases where a spouse or a relative helps with the mask.

Some of the early signs of dementia include:

- Forgetfulness
- Shortened attention span
- Difficulty with simple math
- Difficulty in expressing thoughts
- Changing or unpredictable moods

- Avoiding trying new things or meeting new people
- Confusion and disorientation

Dementia used to be called senility. It is not part of the normal aging process but results from specific diseases. Of the third-age Americans suffering from dementia, about 60 percent have Alzheimer's disease while the remaining 40 percent suffer from other forms of dementia.

I first encountered dementia when a neighbor called me to express concern about Wanda who lived in the other part of a duplex apartment. I knocked on the door, and an exceedingly friendly, attractive woman in her late sixties opened the door. After I explained that I was with a program called Early Intervention for Senior Citizens—I never used the word "mental health center"—Wanda welcomed me inside. "Why of course, come in. Would you like some coffee?" she said. "My husband is in the bathroom. I'll tell him you're here."

For the first ten minutes of our thirty-minute conversation, I questioned the validity of the referral. Wanda carried on a normal conversation, served coffee with grace, and twice asked her husband to come out and meet me. But by the time I left, I had tentatively confirmed the diagnosis of Alzheimer's Disease by the neighbor. Although Wanda handled the social situation perfectly and was a great conversationalist, she displayed symptoms of dementia, which was eventually diagnosed as Alzheimer's disease. She commented five times on my shoes, saying, "My, those are the shiniest shoes I've ever seen." When I asked her age, she gave three different answers, and did not seem to notice that I had asked the same question three times. She had what I call the Alzheimer's look, although the literature never refers to this condition. Many Alzheimer's victims wear a bland stare that is easily discernible. What was most interesting about Wanda was that had she not kept commenting on my shoes or known her age, I might not have considered her "demented," because most of her conversation was appropriate.

Alzheimer's Disease

The onset of Alzheimer's disease, which is the fourth leading cause of death in America, is slow and gradual. The speed with which Alzheimer's disease progresses varies from three to four years in the most rapidly moving cases, six to eight years in average cases, and up to twenty years in slow-moving situations. The most common initial symptom is loss of short-term memory: a victim forgets to turn off a stove or take medication. Sometimes mild personality changes or social withdrawal may occur. As the disease progresses, the victim has difficulty with abstract thinking or doing simple math. He or she may become irritable and ignore personal cleanliness and appearance. Then in latter stages, victims often become confused, disoriented about time, place, the past, and people. Some exhibit psychotic behavior, experiencing delusions and hallucinations. Others become combative. As dementia becomes advanced, the victim stops conversing, becomes erratic in mood, incontinent, unable to care for himself or herself, and stops recognizing family members. It is important to remember that each victim reacts differently, meaning that any of the above symptoms may appear in degrees at almost any stage. Though death can occur in the last stages of Alzheimer's Disease, many victims die earlier from a secondary illness such as pneumonia.

Other Dementias

Alzheimer's disease accounts for 60 percent of dementia; the remaining 40 percent can be accounted for as follows:

- *Multi-infarct dementia.* A series of small strokes, is characterized by deterioration in steps rather than the progressive deterioration of Alzheimer's Disease.

- *Multiple sclerosis.* Over a period of years of mental and physical deterioration, multiple sclerosis destroys the protective covering of the nerve cells.

- *Parkinson's disease.* Causes dementia when the disease is severe or advanced. Parkinson's disease, which becomes worse at a progressive rate, begins with involuntary movements and small tremors.

- *Creutzfeldt-Jakob disease.* Thought to be caused by a viral infection, results in a rapid and progressive dementia.

- *Huntington's disease.* A genetic disorder which begins in middle age, results in a changed personality, mental decline, psychosis, movement disturbance, and lapse into a vegetative state.

Pseudo-Dementias

A family may bring in a client who has all the symptoms of dementia but is suffering from pseudo-dementia, an often treatable condition whose symptoms can be reversed.

Overmedication is the most common cause of reversible dementia. Third-age people sometimes take too many medicines or the medicines may create negative side effects. The metabolism of third-age people is often slower than that younger people; drugs remain in the body longer and when combined with other medication may reach dangerous levels. Competent physicians often prescribe smaller dosages for third-age people because of this possibility.

Chemical imbalances caused by poor nutrition may result in dementia-like symptoms. Because the brain requires a regular supply of proper nutrients, poor eating habits or digestion problems, especially if combined with overmedication, may cause symptoms that resemble those of depression or dementia.

Diseases of the heart or lungs may cause pseudo-dementia. Because the brain requires a great deal of oxygen, if diseased lungs cannot draw enough oxygen into the blood or a diseased heart fails to pump enough blood to the brain, either of these conditions can result in dementia-like behavior.

Diseases of the adrenal, thyroid, pituitary, or other glands that in part regulate emotions, perceptions, memory, and thought processes may result in pseudo-dementia.

Depression also may result in symptoms that resemble those of dementia. People suffering from depression may act confused and respond slowly; not all depressed people appear depressed or act sad.

Dementia Versus Depression

Because the symptoms of dementia and depression sometimes closely resemble one another, make sure you have a clear understanding of the subtle differences (see the chart on the next page).

When you suspect dementia in a client, your first recommendations should be medical and neurological examinations. But even if you only see a client once, remember that one fourth of all Alzheimer's victims are depressed, and about half of Alzheimer's victims have a mixture of Alzheimer's and vascular dementia.

When taking a family history, ask if other family members have suffered from dementia or depression. Estimates of the inheritance of Alzheimer's Disease vary from 5 to 30 percent.

Ask, "Why are you here?"

Dementia	**Depression**
Slow onset	Quick onset
Slow progression	Rapid progression
Previously healthy	Prior health problems
Patients do not complain of cognitive losses	Many complaints
Symptoms often intensify in late afternoon or at night	Symptoms remain independent of environment
Shallow affect	Changeable affect
Quick to answer questions but often incorrect	Answers "I don't know" to many questions

Ask if your client suffered from depression earlier in life.

Ask if your client has suffered major traumatic events in the last few years that might have resulted in depression.

Ask if your client has had erratic sleeping problems.

If you give the mini-mental tests and your client scores less than twenty, something more than depression is involved.

Your last question to your client should be open-ended. "Is there anything else that you want to tell me?"

In the initial interview, consider the following when a spouse, caregiver, or family member is present:

Although questions should be directed to the client, validate the responses by observing the reactions of those who are present. If the client is not responding accurately, the family or caregiver will almost always respond with a negative shake of the head.

Families may not be totally honest with you when the client is in the room. You may wish to interview the family members, spouse, or caregiver alone.

If the family has brought in a client, watch the dynamics of the family together. This can provide an indication of the quality of care your client is receiving.

Ask about the health of the caregiver. This will indicate whether an extended role as caregiver is possible.

Ask about the support system of the victim. Can the family provide needed, long-term support? Watch the caregiver closely. The caregiver may be suffering from dementia or depression.

Alzheimer's disease affects people differently; no two people are ever exactly alike in the disease progression. Although you will be looking for patterns, remember that there are exceptions to any pattern. You may find that a client suspected of depression suffers from dementia and that a client suspected of dementia may be suffering from depression.

During the initial interview take a psychosocial history and look for clues to the concern. Recommend and schedule an extensive medical and neurological examination. If there isn't an Alzheimer clinic in the area that specializes in the diagnosis of Alzheimer's disease and other dementias, work with the family and with the family physician to arrange the tests.

If the diagnosis is dementia, relay this diagnosis to your client and his or her family in a family conference. Expect a multitude of questions about the future.

Schedule another family conference within a week if possible. A week will provide time for the family to think about the ramifications of the diagnosis. After a week, devise a tentative care plan with the client and family.

If you remain involved, arrange to see your client or family every three to six months. Provide counseling for the caregiver should there be a need, and remember the tremendous stress involved in caring for a victim of dementia. Not all caregivers are capable of responding to the demands of caring for a victim of dementia, and you can help by providing the name of a local support group and other support services.

Family Members and Alzheimer's Victims

Following a diagnosis of Alzheimer's disease, you will work far more with the family than with the victim. You can help a victim primarily by making certain your client has medication for depression, delusions, or aggressiveness if that is the case, but your major goal is to provide help to the family by informing the family of available services, options in caring for the victim, and how to best deal with the victim. When I work with the family of a victim, even if I see the family only one time, I have five subject areas that I like to discuss informally with them.

1. The progression of disease

Every family will ask about the speed of deterioration. The average time between the appearance of symptoms and death is usually seven to ten years. Each situation is different, and the time between symptoms and death may be three years for one person and twenty for someone else. Once a pattern of deterioration has been established, a victim usually follows that pattern. Rarely will a victim deteriorate for awhile on a five-year span and then change to a fifteen-year span. Alzheimer's disease is a progressive, degenerative disease that follows a general time frame.

2. The stages of the disease

Alzheimer experts disagree on stages. One expert says there are no stages; another concludes there are six stages. It makes little difference who is more correct. I prefer to divide Alzheimer's disease into three stages—all from the perspective of the family. When the disease begins, the symptoms are relatively minor and the victim can remain at home. This is followed by a stage when the family must seek outside help—a sitter or companion who comes into the home, placing the victim in adult daycare for a few days a week, or placing the victim in a bed-and-board facility. (In our area, we have several relatively good private homes. A caretaker will care for two or three Alzheimer's victims, sometimes for a weekend or a few days a week, or on a full-time basis.) In the final stage, care becomes so demanding that placement in a nursing home is necessary. I always emphasize that at some point the family will have to place the victim in a nursing home. Don't dwell on this aspect, however; I like to plant the idea as a seed. When a family is told that nursing home placement is inevitable, the family can reach that decision with less guilt than might otherwise be the case.

3. Impending personality changes

Families often are not prepared for a change in a victim's personality. They assume that the person will remain the same except for memory problems. While for the most part this is just what happens, at other times the victim becomes someone else. A mild-mannered, soft-spoken man may become an emotional abusive loudmouth, spewing obscenities. On the other hand, a wife or child abuser may become a mild-mannered, soft-spoken, courteous individual. A calm grandmotherly sort may become violent. Make the family aware that this may happen.

4. Alzheimer's disease is a physical illness

Families tend to forget that Alzheimer's is a physical illness. You might compare this disease to a broken leg that not only doesn't heal, but gets worse. The difference is that a broken leg affects just the leg while Alzheimer's disease affects the brain. Because it is a physical disease that affects the brain, instead of feeling guilt the family must learn to deal with the victim differently. It is especially important that family members understand that they cannot argue with or reason with the victim.

5. Protection for the family

A family can deal with the stress of caring for an Alzheimer's victim by understanding the disease. Recommend a good book about living with a victim of Alzheimer's (see Appendix 9). Suggest a support group. If family members are not readers or group oriented, at the very least they need someone to talk with. Remind them that while one person may adapt easily to being a caregiver, someone else may not be able to fill the role. If a family member is not a good caregiver it does not mean there is something wrong with the person. Rather, it just means the victim needs more outside help from caregivers, adult day care, or should be placed in a nursing home earlier.

Point out the decisions that must be made when dealing with an Alzheimer's victim and that they may find it helpful to seek the counsel of others about these decisions.

Give the family your office number. Encourage them to call with questions or to discuss the situation.

Case Studies

Bill and Alice

One of the most tender scenes I've ever witnessed occurred in an Alzheimer's Center. Bill and Alice, both in their early eighties, were scheduled for a three-month evaluation. Bill, who had been diagnosed with Alzheimer's disease six months before, was coming in for his second three-month checkup. The goal was to monitor Bill and estimate the progression of his disease.

Tony, the geriatric psychiatrist, looked at me and smiled. "You'll like Bill and Alice. They're great people."

When Bill and Alice entered the room, Alice walked in first, taking a few steps and then moving her walker forward. Bill followed, moving slowly, not only because Alice was using her walker, but also because she was on oxygen. She had tubes running from her nose to a portable oxygen which Bill was pulling on a little cart.

Despite their health problems, Bill and Alice were a delightful, upbeat couple, laughing and talking freely, engaging in friendly conversation with Tony. I had never met them before, and as I watched Bill, I wondered about the diagnosis of Alzheimer's Disease. This skepticism increased when I recognized Bill. He and I had worked for the same newspaper in the early 1970s. After mentioning this to Bill, he remembered me, and we spent a few minutes reminiscing about the newspaper and about people we knew. His memory of this period of his life twenty years ago was excellent. When Tony gave Bill a mini-mental test, Bill's difficulty began to surface. Bill would answer four or five of the simple questions accurately, then he would supply an off-the-wall answer. Bill knew the day of the week and the month, but when asked the year he responded with "1956." He answered some more questions accurately, but then when asked the name of the President, he said, "Eisenhower." Then Bill and Alice began discussing their lifestyle. Alice, of course, was primarily house-bound because of her health, and Bill, who was still physically active, liked to take a walk every day. Until a month ago, Bill had walked around the block. However, one day he became confused and could not find his way home. Since that day, Bill said he walked in their backyard, and Alice said there had been a couple of times when Bill did not recognize her.

As the interview continued, both Bill and Alice expressed concern about their future. Both realized that Bill's world was becoming progressively smaller, and both wondered what would happen to him if Alice, whose health was tenuous, died first. They discussed this potential situation with great rationality. Both gave us cheerful good-byes as they left to go home—Alice with her walker and Bill pulling the portable oxygen tank.

Sadly, they never had to deal with Bill being left alone; he died three months later.

Sarah

Sarah had lived in her high-rise for four years. For the first three years she lived with her husband Gus, but a year and a half ago he had died. Since then, Sarah's life had been difficult. As a couple, Sarah and Gus had spent their lives living on the proverbial edge. Gus had been an alcoholic, and over the years Sarah, too went through periods when she drank far too much and too often. But they had survived the bad times and lived into their seventies. Then Gus died, leaving Sarah alone.

In the eighteen months since his death, Sarah had been lonely and depressed. The manager of the apartment building noticed other problems. Sarah forgot things. She imagined things that did not happen, she accused Bill, the manager, of striking her.

After Bill called me, at first I assumed Sarah's problem was depression caused by grief for her deceased husband. I soon suspected that other problems were involved. So I made an appointment with our Center psychiatrist and his diagnosis supported my own: that Sarah suffered from both depression and dementia. He prescribed an antidepressant, and I made an appointment to see Sarah in four days. On that day, I asked Sarah if she had been taking her medication. She said she had. When I counted the pills, I discovered that she had not taken one.

I spoke with the manager and explained that Sarah would need help with her medication. Two days later, the manager called me and asked me for help. "I can't deal with her anymore. She's requiring more help than the rest of my residents combined. I counted her pills this morning, and she had only three left. Then I ran up the stairs and found the rest of them spilled on the couch."

I found myself in a critical situation. Sarah could not live alone. Her dementia did not require a nursing home, but her sister was not interested in having Sarah come live with her. I was about to make arrangements for room-and-board, when a brother appeared and volunteered to take Sarah. It was an answer to a difficult situation.

Late Onset Paranoia

Every month or so I receive a call about someone who is convinced that he or she is in danger. Someone or some group is planning harm, watching, stalking, stealing, or rummaging through personal belongings. Often, the family member or social-service organization does not know whether to believe or discount the accusations. Often the accusations contain partial truth. For example, a family of questionable origin may have moved in across the street, or a man may spend considerable time sitting in a nearby car. Regardless of the origin, a person suffering from paranoia will exaggerate a partial truth into a threat.

Common Elements in Late Onset Paranoia

Victims of late onset paranoia, have several elements in common that seem to be present most of the time:

1. The paranoia emerges quickly and without cause.

Most individuals suffering from paranoia enjoyed normal life until the suspicion began. In speaking with families of paranoia victims, I've found that the victim lived a normal life until six months or a year earlier. Then the victim slowly began speaking about the new concern. At first there was a slight suspicion, then the victim began speaking with great conviction. The only deviation from this norm was that maybe twenty per cent of the individuals were described as being suspicious much of their life.

Twice as many women as men suffer from late-onset paranoia, and most of them fall victim in their sixties rather than later in life.

2. The paranoia victim feels tremendous anxiety.

Along with suspicion is a feeling of tremendous anxiety. The victim becomes fixated on the source of suspicion: the man sitting in the car, the group that comes in and tampers with the victim's belongings, the neighbor who is spraying insecticide under the door and through the wall. Whatever the source, the victim feels mounting anxiety. Neither depression nor panic attacks are common, but the combination of suspicion and anxiety has occurred in every situation I encountered.

3. The victim functions relatively well otherwise.

People who suffer from paranoia are not otherwise debilitated. Most keep their house clean, go to the market, attend church, do whatever they did prior to becoming suspicious about something or someone. The one area in which paranoia seems to most affect their lives is in cooking. Some of the paranoia victims I have known were afraid that the person who was after them might have poisoned the food or sabotaged the stove.

Source of Late Onset Paranoia

When the condition continues long enough to rule out a reaction to medication and other more common explanations, most geriatric psychiatrists identify dementia, organic brain deterioration, depression, or unknown causes as the source of a victim's paranoia.

In attempting to help someone with late onset paranoia you can expect only marginal success. While you can treat and cure someone with depression, there is no cure for late onset paranoia. The most you can hope for is to deal with the symptoms by reducing the anxiety.

Medication is the key. Medication may reduce the symptoms of paranoia to a point where your client can live a reasonably normal life. Although the symptoms do not disappear, a mild dose of an antipsychotic drug that works against anxiety can reduce the impact of the symptoms. As with Alzheimer's disease, counseling is of marginal value. All you can do is arrange for medication, work with the family to make certain your client takes the medication, and monitor the client. Performing these tasks effectively can greatly improve your clients' lifestyle.

Case Studies

Anna

Some of the most caring, most perceptive people I have ever met manage senior-oriented apartment buildings. One of my favorite managers called me about a resident whose behavior had been changing over the previous six months. A loner, Anna had spent most of her time quietly in her apartment or outside taking walks and running errands. Then her habits changed, and she began spending hours sitting in the lobby. Anna didn't say anything; she just sat there. When the manager asked her if anything was wrong, Anna shrugged and continued staring at the television.

The manager persisted, and Anna finally described her situation. The apartment building had steam heat and sometimes the heating element made cracking sounds. Anna told the manager that a voice was speaking to her from the heating system. This voice, Anna said, told her not to turn the stove on. As a result, Anna had not been cooking and avoided staying in her apartment because of the voice.

After the manager called me, I quickly arranged a medication appointment with the mental health center psychiatrist. I picked Anna up and drove her to the mental health center, reassuring her constantly that this would require only a few minutes. "I don't like doctors or hospitals," she said several times. But I managed to get her up the back stairs. The psychiatrist talked with her, prescribed mild antipsychotic medication and diagnosed her as having late onset schizophrenia.

The medication helped tremendously. The voice still spoke to Anna from the heating system, but her anxiety level was greatly reduced. She went back to cooking and began associating more with other residents. Instead of speaking in five or six word spurts, she began conversing at length again. The manager continues to watch Anna carefully, and I see her on occasion. If it were not for the watchful manager, I would have to see her far more frequently. Positive change resulted from the medication, and Anna realized that she felt better, so she took the medication as prescribed.

Dorothy

A week later I received a call from a local health clinic about Dorothy. "Dorothy has been coming to us for years," said the head nurse. "Now she says she cannot come to see the doctor. She's afraid to leave the house. She says the people across the street will come in and bother her things." The nurse and I went to see Dorothy and found an anxiety-ridden woman who was friendly to us but fearful of her neighbors.

Dorothy would not leave her house to see the psychiatrist, who I'm certain would have prescribed medication. The psychiatrist would not prescribe medication without seeing Dorothy. We were at an impasse. I did what I could, but Dorothy continued to deteriorate. It soon became obvious that Dorothy could be helped only by hospitalization.

I alerted our crisis people and one Friday night I received a call from a crisis worker. The crisis worker and the police were at Dorothy's house. She had called the police twenty-seven times during the month and they had notified the crisis worker. Dorothy was remanded to the psychiatric ward where she spent ten days. Medication helped and now she lives a normal life. With the help of a supportive family, she takes her medication on schedule.

Chapter 11

Suicide, Terminal Illness, and Traumatic Experiences

Suicide

Counselors who work with third-age people rarely work with people who are seriously contemplating suicide. Third-age people in this frame of mind often withdraw and refuse to discuss their feelings. When someone is suicidal, calls are often made to crisis centers that are staffed with people trained to work with these cases. However, even though you will not see much evidence of suicide potential in your clients, it does not diminish the threat to third-age people.

During the last two decades, the suicide rate of those sixty-five plus has increased. H.L.P. Resnick and J.M. Cantor found in 1970 that people over sixty committed 25 percent of all suicides. That rate has increased until today the suicide rate of this age population is almost twice that of the rest of the population.

Active and Passive Suicidal Thought

Active suicidal thinking occurs when a person dwells on method. Although not everyone who actively thinks about suicide follows through, enough people in their third age do take their own lives to create this age-population's high suicide rate. Despite this, I am called in on an emergency suicide no more than once a year. I assume this is because people who are serious about suicide do not talk about it to family or ask for the intervention of counselors.

Passive suicidal thinking is reflected in statements like: "I just wish I were dead." "Every night when I go to bed I hope I don't wake up in the morning." "I just wish something would happen to me." A person in this frame of mind is not actively considering taking his or her life. Such statements denote a state of depression and once the depression leaves, the person wants to continue living. I have encountered people who utter suicidal words and feel this way but are not really depressed. People in this state of mind have rationally decided that they have had enough of life, are displeased with life as it is, and are ready to die.

One client whom I still see periodically, rationally decided he wanted to die. Andrew was in his mid-eighties, and had lost his wife a dozen years earlier. As he aged, his activities were curtailed. His family physician prescribed a very appropriate antidepressant. I did everything that I could to help Andrew, but without success. He erected a roadblock to every suggestion because he simply had no desire to continue living. I'm not sure that he ever seriously considered suicide, yet if his obituary were to appear in tomorrow's newspaper, I would wonder about the cause.

Facts about Third-Age Suicide

The suicide rate for males continues to increase with age, even into the seventies and eighties. With females, there is a slight decrease in the rate of suicide beginning in the fifties.

Although third-age people are less likely than younger people to attempt suicide, when third-age people do attempt suicide they are more likely to be successful. Third-age people are less likely to use suicidal gestures as a manipulative ploy or cry for help, and third-age people are less likely to be rescued from a suicide attempt.

The possibility of suicide seems to increase in certain lifestyle situations. The widowed are more likely to commit suicide than those whose spouses are living. Those who have been forced to retire contemplate suicide more than those who voluntarily retired. Although poor health, living alone, alcohol abuse, and similar stresses are related to suicide in the elderly, suicide attempts result more from an accumulation of events and circumstances over a prolonged period of time than from a specific, emotionally upsetting event. A 1991 study by David Clark in Chicago found that older suicide victims had experienced relatively few high-stress events like the death of a spouse, economic ruin, and isolation. Instead, those who committed suicide were more likely to be emotionally disturbed; 65 percent were depressed and 19 percent were alcoholic.

Dealing with the Person in Crisis

You can work months without encountering a person who seriously contemplates suicide, but when you do, you should know how to handle it. Whether talking on the telephone, sitting across the room from the person in an office, or sitting in the person's home, follow this general approach:

1. Remain calm.

Maintain equanimity no matter how agitated or emotional your client is. By speaking calmly, by reacting non-judgmentally, you can help soothe the potential victim.

2. Encourage your client to talk.

Someone contemplating suicide often has withdrawn from the rest of the world. Because of this isolation, your client may be ready to talk. By encouraging this, you allow the person to ventilate, to pour out his or her problems. It also gives you the opportunity to examine the nature of the suicide threat. There is a big difference between a person thinking something and saying those thoughts out loud. Speaking the words allows your client to examine the content of the thoughts.

3. Ask if your client is considering injuring himself or herself and, if so, find out if a plan exists.

There is a difference between wishing life would end and having a plan to end life. The more concrete and elaborate the plan, the greater the risk of suicide. Potential victims who have methodically put their affairs in order are at great risk, for they have given thought to the specifics of death. Their threat to harm themselves is serious.

4. Seek out the concern behind the suicidal threat.

With younger people, suicide may be contemplated because of a specific event: a relationship that fell apart, a career that has not flourished, or any of a thousand other specific events. Although a specific situation may trigger suicidal thoughts in a third-age person, more often this threat follows a succession of losses: difficulty adjusting to retirement, loss of work friendships, health problems, loss of a spouse. The potential victim may be able to deal with each loss individually, but when they occur concurrently or within a few years, that person may believe he or she can no longer deal with the compounding stresses of life.

5. Seek out your client's strengths.

People contemplating suicide have hit lows in their lives. Everything negative seems to be happening at once, or a string of negative events has damaged self esteem. Strengths have been forgotten or overlooked in attempting to deal with this series of losses. Gently probe until these strengths are discovered. After discovering your client's personal strengths, offer your client a more balanced look at the world.

6. Provide options to the situation facing the victim.

People pondering suicide believe it is the most logical way to deal with problems. Spend time brainstorming, and looking for options, as a means of convincing a potential victim that there is another way of dealing with those problems. Offering options does not mean giving advice. A family member might say, "Sleep on it. You'll feel better in the morning." You can make the same observation, but frame it in another way. I told a potential victim: "When we are upset, we tend to look at the world through distorted glasses. Sometimes a little time lets us see things more clearly." Provide a potential victim with "what ifs."

7. When possible, end the session with a plan, an informal contract.

One night I received an early morning call on the mental health center crisis line from a young man who was seriously considering taking his life. We spent an hour-and-a-half following the steps outlined above. Before we ended the conversation, I said, "Jeff, let's make certain we both understand how you're going to spend the next twenty-four hours. You're going to lie down and try to sleep. Then tomorrow morning, you'll call the mental health center for an appointment. Agreed?" Jeff agreed. By ending the session with a plan, an agreement, a contract, you attempt to lock in a potential victim to a course of action other than suicide.

Although these general principles may help you with a potential suicide victim, never forget that you also have the option of calling in backup. Most mental health centers have people who have been trained in dealing with potential suicide victims. Don't hesitate to call in a mental health center worker or encourage a potential victim to go to a hospital emergency room, which will then contact a mental health center crisis team.

I usually visit a just-released client at least twice a week for a couple of weeks. Almost all patients of psychiatric wards are released with medication, so attempt to ascertain that the client is taking the prescribed medication, that the medication is working, and that there are no major side effects from that medication. Some people lack the understanding of the importance of psychiatric medication and cease taking the medication at the first opportunity. During this stage of recovery, medication may be the primary obstruction to a relapse.

In addition to providing twice weekly and then weekly counseling sessions, provide your suicidal client with support. Your clients should understand that should they begin sliding back into thinking about hurting themselves they can call you. Some third-age people live a lonely, isolated life. Knowing there is someone to call when thoughts turn to suicide provides considerable relief.

As part of the counseling process, work with your client to examine the cause or string of losses that contributed to the consideration of suicide. Although sometimes all you and your client can do in the process is talk about the cause, other times a more direct approach can be used. If the problem is financial, perhaps a move to a high-rise might be in order. Most apartment buildings for third-age people rent on a sliding scale, which usually leaves the client with a larger discretionary income. Regardless of the cause, the counseling process should focus on the primary cause that led to the suicidal thinking.

Case Studies

Jean Marie

Jean Marie had been married twice, once to a man she described as a "louse" and a second time to a "good man, but we couldn't get along." (She was friendly with her second husband and his wife.) After her two children were in school, she worked in a factory for twenty-two years until it closed. She then worked at minimum wage jobs while taking night courses at the local community college, where she earned an associate degree in social service.

During the next five years she worked at almost every social service agency in the area. She would work at one agency for six months or a year, become dissatisfied, and begin working at another agency. Jobs were plentiful during this period. On weekends, she would attend various arts and crafts shows and sell the ribbon crafts that she made in her spare time.

Then the employment picture changed. Because of tighter budgets in the field, people stopped changing jobs as frequently. Jean Marie, who had been very verbal in the workplace and criticized agencies for inefficiency, found that because of her past record and the change in the employment market, she could not get a job. For three years she worked at temporary jobs outside the social service field, surviving primarily on a $210 pension from her factory job and from her weekend outings to the craft fairs.

During these three years, she sent out resumes and received well-meaning advice from friends and family. No one seemed to understand why Jean Marie could not get a job. She became more anxious and more depressed. She had difficulty dealing with the subtle criticism of those around her. Her circle of friends did not understand that she was almost sixty with just two years of college and was competing directly with applicants who had recently graduated.

Jean Marie began thinking of suicide. She was not considering suicide in the immediate future, but it became an option for her. She began thinking about how she might do it. She picked out a specific tree if she was going to have an auto accident. She considered pills. She considered closing the garage and starting her car.

I received a referral to interview Jean Marie from the manager of a local agency that found part-time work for people fifty-five plus. The manager said that Jean Marie was "a bundle of nerves. I don't know what's going to happen to her. She cannot go on like this much longer."

At the urging of the manager, Jean Marie came into the mental health center for an appointment. She explained her situation. Together we commiserated about the poor job market for someone with her skills. She was competing for the few available jobs with people who had bachelor degrees, and she more than likely was encountering age discrimination.

It was an obvious problem-solving situation: if Jean Marie could find a job, her frustration would disappear. We began brainstorming about the job market; then I became curious about how she was supporting herself.

She said that she owned her house, she had her pension, and that she made enough from her crafts fairs to live.

My next suggestion was that if income was not a major issue, perhaps she could look at her situation differently. Perhaps she could upgrade her crafts selling and consider it a small business. Also, she might consider herself as just treading water until she was old enough to receive Social Security. With this perspective, she would not have to deal with the frustration incurred from fruitless job hunting.

With these suggestions, Jean Marie's perspective changed immediately. "That's wonderful. That's what I really want to do. But you're the first person who said it was okay." I never again met with Jean Marie. When I called her a month later, she said everything was wonderful.

Sometimes we are so influenced by other people and by society that we ignore our own desires. Jean Marie needed permission from someone to follow her wishes. Her circle of family and friends had decided that Jean Marie could not live without a job. A counselor, who has the advantage of working from outside of a person's circle of friends and family, can sometimes counter the pressure of this circle with the right observation.

Harry and Maude

Before Maude met Harry, life was difficult for her. Maude's childhood had been unpleasant. She married an abuser. Then she spent fifteen years alone. At age fifty-eight she met Harry, who was two years older and had been divorced for a decade. When they met chemistry took over. They married a few months later.

The next fifteen years proved to be as happy and delightful as both had hoped. Then, when Maude was seventy-three and Harry was seventy-five, disaster destroyed their happiness. Harry became ill with terminal cancer and was given only a few months to live. When Harry fell ill, Maude became almost instantly suicidal. She decided that if Harry was going to die, she wanted to die also.

When I pointed out to Maude that Harry's last few months would be difficult and that he needed her support, she cast aside her threats of suicide and provided that support. She was constantly at his side. When Harry died several months later, Maude moved to another state to be near her daughter. I learned of Maude's death less than a year thereafter. Although she died a natural death, it was obvious that she had lost her will to live and probably willed herself to die. She believed that life without Harry was not worth living.

When a person loses the will to live, it's a kind of passive suicide. I have seen several clients like Maude: they decide against active suicide but hope, even pray they will die. Although sometimes you can reach a client with this attitude, at other times the mindset is so strong that no one can help.

Terminal Illness

You may be asked to work with terminally ill people or with the families of these individuals, although usually hospital social workers, nurses, and hospice specialists deal with the terminally ill. However, you may be called in to help individuals or families requiring help coping with the serious stresses that accompany terminal illness.

Feelings and Beliefs About Death

What does an eighty-seven-year-old person feel about approaching death? Research indicates that people in this age of life have some common feelings about death:

- Some do not fear death the same way they feared death when they were younger. They believe that they have lived a long life and understand that life is a process—that people are born, live, and die. Those who have suffered the loss of a spouse or other significant losses may have lost their zeal for living. Individuals with strong beliefs about an afterlife anticipate death, believing that in the afterlife they will connect with loved ones who died before them.

- Some people exercise some control over when they die. Emil told me about the death of his father, Walter, who had developed cancer while in his eighties. When it became obvious that he was losing the battle, Walter arranged for all his family and friends to visit him on a particular Sunday. The father, family, and friends had a great Sunday together. The father was laughing and joking. He talked to everyone and seemed in great spirits. Then, that evening, after everyone had left, he turned to his son and said, "I'm ready to go now." He died the next day.

The more secure and stable people are, the less they fear death. This is a personal belief and to my knowledge has never been substantiated by research. People who grow up with more than the ordinary amount of insecurities and who live disastrously uncomfortable lives spend their lives fearing what might happen. So, too, they fear death in an abnormal way. They become so preoccupied with the fear of death that they live half a life. A stable person lives his or her time living a vital life without becoming preoccupied with fears of death.

There are two kinds of terminal illness: *acknowledged* and *unacknowledged*.

With *acknowledged* terminal illness, everyone knows that a patient has a limited amount of time left. *Unacknowledged* terminal illness concerns a person who may have a few months, a few years, or even a few decades left, but the person and the family live with a kind of time bomb waiting to go off. Unacknowledged terminal illness creates unique pressures.

The family of a terminal patient tries to live a normal life, knowing that an illness may result in death at any time. In the event of cancer, everyone hopes that treatment, often chemotherapy or radiation, will place the disease into permanent remission. But when cancer returns the second time, the victim and the family realize but often do not acknowledge that the illness will bring death. The victim, spouse, or other family members live with the additional pressure of watching for symptoms that the cancer has returned. Although some families discuss the situation, other families pretend it does not exist. They discuss future plans, knowing these plans more than likely will never be realized.

Some families and victims cannot cope with the pressures that accompany terminal illness, and react in a variety of ways. Some people become depressed. Spouses may leave their mates for other reasons, when in reality they cannot deal with the pressure of their partners' impending death. Some victims lead wild, irrational lives, while others live almost cloistered lives, giving up and preparing to die. Often the family of the victim has more difficulty than the victim, who may have made peace with the situation.

Terminal Illness Counseling

When you are asked to help someone with either an acknowledged or unacknowledged terminal illness, you can provide solace and support in these ways:

- Help the victim and family place the illness and time left in perspective. Offer axioms like, "live each day to the fullest" and "live one day at a time."

- Provide empathic support to client and family by being available to them, verbalizing empathic support, and listening to and supporting them in their concerns.

- To the degree that it is possible, follow the wishes of the terminally ill client. If necessary, inform the client of details of the illness and help the client talk about all facets of the illness.

- Help preserve a positive relationship between client and family and the hospital staff by facilitating communication between all concerned.

- Allow the person to die with dignity. A victim's choice of how to die should be respected. If it is the client's wish, help to insure that his or her life is not prolonged through intrusive resuscitations or life extension efforts.

- Help the client to mourn, to discuss his or her past life, and support beliefs in immortality and any other spiritual beliefs.

- Encourage a life review in which the client reviews past achievements and takes care of unfinished business.

- Explain to the client and family the legal options open to them, such as a durable power of attorney for health care, or a living will.

- Help a victim and family resolve the displaced emotions such as anger or blame that often arise in coping with the stresses of terminal illness.

- Try to adjust to any reasonable needs and desires of the terminally ill client and family.

Case Studies

Ardeth

Ardeth was a late bloomer. An African-American woman, her childhood had been difficult. She had married early in life and bore three children by the time she was twenty. Her husband worked in a factory and provided Ardeth and her children with a decent living, but there was no warmth in her life. By the time Ardeth was thirty-five, she was an alcoholic. She spent a dozen years in an alcoholic stupor, then surfaced in her late forties.

When Ardeth decided to straighten out her life, she acted quickly. She earned a bachelor's and a master's degree in social work. She served several years as a social worker and, a month after being accepted into a Ph.D. program, Ardeth, now in her late fifties, was diagnosed with cancer. Cancer had started in her lungs and spread to her brain. (It was the probable result of years of heavy cigarette smoking.) She was given six months to live.

As a favor to a friend, I visited Ardeth in the hospital. Although in the midst of debilitating treatment for her cancer, Ardeth revealed a strong desire to live. She talked primarily of continuing in the Ph.D. program. This aspect of her struggle did not come to fruition, for she was never able to return to school or work again. But she never gave up the battle and was still alive six years later.

The friend who asked me to counsel Ardeth had underestimated her strength. Ardeth didn't need me. The will to live is an almost indefinable quality that can be either present or absent. I have seen people whose bodies have been worn out for years but who are determined to retain each possible breath of life. Other people lose this will to live rather easily: it does not take much to make some people give up.

Harley

Harley was a seventy-four-year-old man who had ignored all the rules of healthful living. When he retired, he ate sausages and eggs for breakfast and red meat with his other two meals. His exercise consisted of several trips to and from the bedroom and living room to the table. After ten years of abusing his body, he had gained a hundred pounds, could barely walk, and found out that all the arteries to his heart were 70 to 90 percent blocked.

I was asked by Harley's wife, whom I already knew, to help them make a decision. They needed to decide if Harley should have by-pass surgery. He was told that without the surgery he probably would not live long. He had also been told that if he opted for surgery, there was a chance he would not survive due to his weight and poor condition.

We had a forty-minute session in which we explored the pros and cons of surgery. My role was to help facilitate their discussion of Harley's situation, to help them sort out the choices. When I left, he was seriously considering the operation. A few days later I heard that he had decided against surgery.

Two months later he died of a massive heart attack.

Traumatic Experiences

People undergo negative experiences that vary from the merely uncomfortable to the most serious level of trauma. Most people live their lives without having a truly devastating traumatic experience. The unexpected loss of a significant person is commonly experienced as truly traumatic. It happens so unexpectedly that it devastates and dominates the survivor. However, some experiences may assume a traumatic level for one person while another person experiences it as being merely difficult.

For the most part, stress becomes traumatic when an experience occurs without warning, when an experience seems overwhelming, and when people are unable to tolerate or deal with the experience. People who experience traumatic reactions manifest some or all of the following characteristics:

1. They experience dissociation.

Sometimes the negative experience so devastates a person that he or she stands outside of his or her body and watches what happens. Many victims report feeling out of their body, indicating that this may be a common coping mechanism that protects them from experiences that are too overwhelming to integrate in the moment.

2. The experience is imprinted on their memory.

Countless movies and television shows depict a person who has forgotten a traumatic experience or blocked it out. Although this does occur, more often a person relives the experience over and over, both in thoughts and in nightmares. Reliving continues as an undigested experience until the experience is integrated.

3. They experience a biphase response.

During a traumatic event the body releases chemicals that help the person deal with the emergency. Afterwards, when a person encounters any situation that releases the same chemicals, the victim may again relive the traumatic experience.

4. They experience many flashbacks of the event.

The person is constantly reminded of the painful event. There are so many painful memories that the victim cannot avoid thinking of the event. Anything may trigger the victim's recall. The result is an intrusion upon his or her thinking that occasions a personal numbing. In order to deter this intrusion and numbing victims may avoid talking about what happened, avoid being consoled, or simply withdraw from the world.

5. They experience a disruption of the self.

After experiencing a traumatic event, assumptions may be shattered, and the victim feels terribly vulnerable. Victims often lose all feeling about who or what they are; their very identities are disrupted.

6. They experience a loss of trust and safety.

Loss of faith often appears in victims. Some individuals no longer trust or feel safe with other people, who now feel they must earn the trust of the victim. When there is a loss of trust, the victim often withdraws from the world, sometimes into a world of his or her own making.

Helping People Recover from a Traumatic Event

Encourage clients who have suffered traumatic events to talk about the event. By engaging in what might be called talk therapy, you suggest that your client paint a picture with words of what happened. This puts the situation in perspective and relieves a victim's inner stress and turmoil.

By describing the story in detail, your client validates the happening. Clients who do not tell the story in detail will continue to be tortured. They need to talk about what happened and validate the hurt. As you listen, your clients more fully recognize what the hurt and the suffering has done to them. Encourage discussion of the event in order for your clients to legitimize the incident and more fully acknowledge the emotions that accompanied the trauma.

Help your clients realize that healing and recovery requires time. As they remember the past and recount it in a counseling setting, the memory of what happened will change. Initially, clients will remember the tortured past with great intensity; eventually the intensity with which they remember the event will decrease. In time, this intense, torturous event will become a painful memory.

Case Studies

Marge

I was sitting at my desk one morning drinking a cup of coffee when I received a telephone call from Marge. "Mr. Warnick, my friend Grace thinks I should talk with you." Marge spoke very calmly, providing no indication of her crisis.

I made an appointment to visit Marge in about two hours. When I arrived at the high-rise where she lived, she calmly led me into her living room and served coffee. Then she sat down opposite me, and began trembling and shaking as she told me that, on the previous evening, she had gotten into a shoving match with another resident.

For two hours I sat and listened to Marge tell her story at least a dozen times. All I did was restate, on occasion, that she had experienced a traumatic incident and validate that she was justified in feeling anxious and upset. I assured her that she would return to normal within a day or so. I went back two days later to check on Marge, and she was fine. She had returned to normal and had the incident in perspective.

This was a low-level trauma, more of an upsetting experience than a traumatic event, but to Marge it had the characteristics of trauma. Had she not had the opportunity to talk about her feelings, it might have continued to cause her problems.

Crystal

A colleague of mine worked with Crystal following a terrible experience that occurred five years ago and I helped her through what might be called a relapse. Crystal and her husband had lived in a small town north a city where the typical crime entailed a wayward teenager breaking into a store to steal a few dollars.

Then, five years ago, Crystal and her husband Gregory returned home to encounter two young males emerging from their bedroom. They were robbed, and the robbers remained in their home for more than two hours, threatening them while systematically looting their home.

The robbery upset them, but when Crystal could not get over it, she came to our center for help. The counselor recognized Crystal's extreme agitation and arranged for Crystal to get some medication. She saw Crystal three times a week for awhile and then once a week.

Crystal regained her equilibrium, but when she had health problems five years later, the painful intensity of the experience returned. The strategy remained the same as before: arrange for medication, lead Crystal through the experience step by step, and provide the support and validation she required.

Because of the intensity of the traumatic experience, I don't know if Crystal has conquered her painful memories of that event, or if difficulties will appear again should Crystal experience another crisis. If her memories do emerge again, Crystal has learned that brief treatment will help her deal with a periodic crisis.

Chapter 12

Ten Case Studies

C ounselors of third-age people encounter a gamut of unique situations. Here are ten such case examples. As with all clients, the degree of success I was able to achieve depended largely upon the motivation of the client.

Dorothy

Dorothy had lived for several years in high-rises and had a reputation for being friendly and cooperative, except for what everyone described as "spells." These spells were not like seizures in that, for a few days Dorothy would become very emotional and speak of dreams that bothered her, alienating those around her so that they avoided her. Then she would return to normal until the next "spell."

When I arrived at work one morning, I had a message awaiting me from a high-rise building manager. He had spent much of the night trying to deal with Dorothy, who was highly emotional and babbling incoherently. The manager had called our crisis hot line, and the man on call spent an hour listening to Dorothy. "I don't know what her problem is," the very competent mental health worker said, "but it looks like either dementia or paranoid schizophrenia." An additional problem was that Dorothy's religion prohibited hospitalization or the taking of medication. "Regardless what her problem is," the crisis worker continued, "she needs to go to the psychiatric ward."

I went out to the high-rise feeling wary and wondering what to do with someone who had become seriously mentally ill but would not take medication or enter a hospital. Because I don't usually deal with people who are seriously mentally ill, I don't feel especially competent in this area. The one or two people I place in the psych ward each year usually have lost control of their depression or anxiety or have suffered late onset paranoia.

I found a slightly different person from the woman who had talked with our crisis worker and had babbled almost incoherently about headless people and other things that did not make much sense. The Dorothy I saw did not babble but could not finish a sentence. In the hour I spoke with her, she could not complete a thought. "I want you to understand that…" "Why don't you…" "I wish I…" Both the manager and the crisis worker had mentioned how upset Dorothy had been about the Waco tragedy involving the Branch Davidians a few days earlier, but when I mentioned this event, Dorothy was unable to complete a sentence describing her thoughts.

Everyone who had seen Dorothy had believed that hospitalization was required, and this was also my opinion. But her religion prohibited it. To buy some time while I pondered how to deal with the situation, I suggested to Dorothy that she try to sleep. "Dorothy, I know the Branch Davidian tragedy upset you. You probably haven't slept well since then. So you go in and try to sleep. I'll return in the afternoon and see how you're feeling." I spoke with several people during the ensuing few hours; no one had any great ideas for dealing with Dorothy's plight. I believed her problem was either dementia, a mental illness such as late onset schizophrenia, or sleep deprivation. When I left the high-rise, I strongly suspected dementia. Four hours later I returned to the high-rise with a co-worker who had spent years dealing with severe, chronic mental illness. To our surprise, Dorothy was up and dressed. She met us at the front door and seemed normal. The person with the dysfunctional mind had disappeared. This was the most surprising change I had seen in all my years in the mental health field. I finally decided that sleep deprivation was responsible for her incoherency. The Waco tragedy had upset her. She had not slept. Without sleep, she exhibited psychotic symptoms. This also explained her other spells. Something would upset her, and she would go a couple of nights without sleep; sleep deprivation would affect her thinking processes. Now Dorothy and I have an arrangement: when something upsets her, she calls me, and I help quiet her so that she can sleep.

Mabel

Mabel had been coming to the mental health center periodically over the course of ten years. She would come in for awhile, receive treatment, and then disappear for several years. She didn't have any major problems; things just happened that would not allow her to cope. Then she called again one day, maintaining that she suffered from agoraphobia and had not left her mobile home for five years.

When I visited her the first time, I found that her retired husband and two of her daughters were caring for her. She would awaken at six o'clock in the morning, and her husband would bring her coffee. She would loll on the bed until nine, and then she would dress and walk to the living room to watch her favorite game show. She would spend the day sitting in her chair watching game shows and CNN, leaving her chair only when she went to the bathroom and to the kitchen table for a lunch her husband prepared.

She stated several times that she disliked living this restricted lifestyle. With this stated position, we designed a plan that would allow her to return to a more normal lifestyle. We arranged a schedule based on systematic desensitization, an approach that has been effective in dealing with agoraphobia. On the first week, we would sit on the porch of her mobile home. On the second week, we would walk in the yard. On the third week we would walk down to the corner of the street. The progression would continue until the tenth week, when we would have coffee at a local restaurant.

The first week went well. The second week found us walking in the yard, but we had to return to the mobile home in a few minutes because Mabel's legs hurt. Still, she hadn't felt nervous at all. Then we began comparing notes and jointly decided that much of her problem resulted from her legs being totally out of condition due to inactivity. We revised the program and decided first to get her legs in shape.

But Mabel did not follow through with her exercises. Each week she had a different excuse. After a month of floundering, we agreed that she really did not care enough about leaving her mobile home to continue our work. She discontinued participation in the program, and I noted that she was so satisfied with her life, with being cared for and catered to by her husband and daughters, that she had no incentive to change.

Bob

Bob's daughter Lillian brought Bob into the crisis center after he threatened suicide. He had held a butcher knife against his throat. Bob was an almost illiterate railroad worker. He was hard of hearing, had lost his wife three years ago, and lived in a tiny house half a block from Lillian.

Bob's main problem involved finances. Although he had good insurance with the railroad and had signed up for Medicare, he had not purchased supplemental insurance. In the year after he retired, he had suffered two major illnesses that resulted in unpaid medical bills due to his lack of insurance.

He was deluged with calls from hospitals and physicians' offices, along with the normal threats that accompanied each bill. It was simply more than he could deal with.

Because I suspected Bob's major problem was concern over his medical bills, I sought first to straighten this out. I went to his major creditors and found out exactly how much he owed: after Medicare paid its share, he owed about $2,000, far less than he and his daughter suspected. I explained to Bob and his daughter that they could pay off these bills in thirty-six installments just like buying a car and be free in three years. I got grudging agreement for this plan from all his creditors. I made certain that Bob bought supplemental insurance.

When I returned to see Bob a couple of days later, he was fine. He no longer had his worries, though he didn't say a word. Tears came to his eyes and he reached up and patted my shoulder. That was his way of saying thanks. This was one of the most touching experiences I have ever had as the counselor.

Blanche

A neighbor called because she was concerned about Blanche, a woman in her seventies who had given away her dog. Blanche had doted on the dog, and the neighbor, knowing that Blanche had severe health problems, feared that Blanche might be considering suicide.

When there is even a hint of suicide, counselors at the mental health center respond quickly. Two hours later, I was knocking on Blanche's door. In her small, one-car garage that had been converted into an efficiency apartment, I found piles of everything. Finding a place to sit down was difficult. I had barely sat down and explained my purpose when Blanche began talking nonstop for two-and-a-half hours. She was not suicidal. Rather, she had regretfully given away her dog because she could no longer care for it. Although she was not suicidal, she was indeed a troubled person. As often happens, this woman's trouble began years ago with her family.

Amid all the piles and clutter, was a large three-foot by four-foot portrait of a distinguished looking man. Painted years ago, the portrait had probably cost lots of money. "This is my father," Blanche said. The garage apartment contained evidence of a far more opulent lifestyle: candlestick holders, vases, and the like. As she told her story, it became clear that her father Bartholomew, whose portrait she cherished, was responsible for her anguish.

She had been born into a wealthy family. Bartholomew owned a chain of successful retail stores. Blanche grew up in the business and after graduating from high school began working for her dad. Blanche fell in love and married a young man who worked in one of the stores. Bartholomew was furious; he had other goals for his only daughter. Although Blanche and her husband continued working in the family business, they suffered Bartholomew's wrath. He treated them with scorn.

Blanche and her husband had two children, a daughter and a son. As the children grew up, Blanche's father became attached to them. When the daughter was in high school Bartholomew made a new will stipulating that if Blanche were to get a share of the inheritance, her daughter had to graduate from college and marry from a list of half a dozen potential husbands, all supplied by Bartholomew. If his granddaughter did not follow his wishes, Bartholomew said he would leave all his wealth to the son and ignore Blanche.

Blanche's daughter grew up, graduated from college, and married a fine young man, though not one from the father's list. (The marriage remains intact today.) Always a man of his word, Bartholomew left all his wealth to his son. This anecdote relates only part of the damage that a domineering father did to a daughter, damage that lasted a lifetime.

Blanche allowed me to see her only that one time. "I may call you some day," she said.

Joyce

Four years before I met Joyce, she went through a very difficult period. Depressed after a late-life divorce, Joyce had money problems and a son with major problems of his own. She became so distressed that she attempted suicide. My predecessor worked very effectively with Joyce, and they worked things out. However, from almost my first day at the center Joyce would show up for help. Every six months she would come back for a three-session booster shot. "I don't ever want to get down as low as I was," she told me.

We managed well for a year. On the occasions when Joyce felt concerned, a few sessions would quell her anxiety. But one day Joyce said, "I feel I'm slipping." Her family physician had been prescribing psychiatric medication. When I saw the deterioration begin, I urged Joyce to let me make an appointment with the center psychiatrist. Joyce refused. An unbelievably nice woman, Joyce did not want her physician to believe she lacked confidence in him.

The deterioration continued. We increased our sessions to twice weekly. I urged Joyce to see our psychiatrist. She refused. Then one day I received a call: "Jim, I've taken some pills." She had attempted suicide. Joyce spent a week in the hospital. Since her release a year ago, she has been doing fine. But now she sees the center psychiatrist every couple of months. He prescribes medication for her because the medication her family physician prescribed medication did not effectively help her.

Both Joyce and I believe her last episode could have been prevented. Family physicians know comparatively little about psychiatric medication. Granted, family physicians prescribe the bulk of antidepressants and anti-anxiety medications, and they usually make reasonably effective decisions. If family physicians did not prescribe these medications, most individuals would simply go home and suffer because many people still balk at the idea of seeing a psychiatrist. But a family physician should realize that at a certain point it's best to refer the client to a psychiatrist.

Monica

The manager of a local high-rise asked me to see Monica, who had lived in the high-rise for almost ten years. Recently Monica had complained that neighbors on each side were spraying Raid through the wall. When I visited Monica, she cautioned me against speaking too loudly. She said her neighbors were listening. She also pointed out what she said was a redness in her television picture.

Monica believed her neighbors were spraying Raid through the television set. As I continued to see her, she came up with new examples of what her neighbors were doing to her.

I consulted the psychiatrist about Monica. He said that more than likely counseling would not help Monica, that only medication would provide relief from her paranoia. But although I saw Monica for the full fourteen sessions I could not convince her to go to the doctor with me. "I don't take any medicine but aspirin," she always said. Because she was on the brink of being evicted, she stopped complaining about the spraying of Raid. I still hear from her periodically and hope that one day she will consent to visit the psychiatrist with me.

Lorridean

When Lorridean began having stomach pains, she went to the physician she had been seeing for years. He examined her, found nothing wrong, and then asked, "Lorridean, is something bothering you?" Lorridean shook her head, but the doctor did not believe her. "Lorridean, I've been your doctor for thirty-five years. You've been having these pains for nine months now. I suggest you seek counseling."

Although I was the first counselor she had ever talked with, she had no difficulty describing the cause of her distress. She was an active seventy-three year old with two brothers. Theodore was in a veterans' home with advanced Parkinson's disease. Her other brother, Vincent, an active eighty-two-year-old, had always been the leader of the family. A retired minister, he had been a source of comfort to her throughout her life.

When her husband had died, Vincent had been there for her. About once a month, Lorridean and Vincent drove a hundred miles to the veterans' home to see Theodore. He was probably beyond recognizing them, but both Lorridean and Vincent felt better after visiting him. Then something happened that upset Lorridean. It started out with Vincent talking about sex. This shocked Lorridean, for he had never done this before. With each trip, Vincent became more graphic in his description. And then on the last trip, Vincent had asked Lorridean to have sex with him.

"Why would he do something like that?" Lorridean asked over and over in our subsequent meetings. Because she refused to allow me to call her brother, I could only provide her with my supposition: that this change in behavior resulted from a physical condition.

We handled the situation this way: I worked with Lorridean to help her understand that something strange was happening to her brother and that she had done nothing to provoke his behavior. She had to make Vincent understand that she would not tolerate any discussion of this sort again. She explained her position to her brother and then refused to be alone with him or to make monthly sojourns to visit Theodore.

Three months after this confrontation, Vincent asked to talk with her. He apologized. They both cried. Their relationship became more normal. But I warned Lorridean against becoming too trusting of him.

Charlie

Charlie was a 103-year-old man who lived alone in his house. Despite his advanced years, he managed reasonably well. A woman from a local home service agency came in once a week to clean his house and five days a week he rode a small bus to a nearby high-rise where he ate lunch with the residents. Recently he'd begun encountering problems. Because he wore the same suit every day and refused to bathe, he smelled so badly that the people on the bus and at the high-rise did not want him near them. The home service agency called upon me to help persuade him to attend to his hygiene.

The most difficult part of dealing with Charlie was getting in to talk with him. He left his hearing aid turned off most of the time. I would go to the back door and see him sitting at his kitchen table, but no matter how hard I pounded or how loud I yelled, he didn't hear me. Finally, on the third visit, he looked up and saw me. He turned on his hearing aid and we discussed the problem.

Because I was reasonably certain that Charlie was getting along fine except for needing a change in his hygiene habits, I only spent about twenty minutes with him. I related the complaint. Then I pointed out that if it was important to him to ride the bus and to eat with the other residents, he had to modify his ways. He had to allow the home service agency to send his suit to the cleaners periodically and to allow the representative to help him bathe.

"Okay," he said. He accepted the changes, and now he rides the bus and eats in the high-rise dining room without problem.

People forget that life is a trade-off, a lifetime compromise. To achieve certain goals, we must provide something in return. Third-age people understand this, for they have been making compromises all their lives. If riding the bus and eating in the dining room had not been important to him, Charlie would still be wearing his smelly suit and refusing to bathe. But it was important to him and so he compromised.

The Winebergs

I returned a call to a social worker whose clinic did Alzheimer diagnostic assessments. "I have a family in need of some help." The Winebergs had just been in for normal tests and had spent an hour-and-a-half yelling at one another. The family included Loretta, an eighty-three-year-old grandmother; Marcena, her fifty-two-year-old daughter; and John, her twenty-nine-year-old grandson. Marcena was on one side and Loretta and John on the other.

John and his two boys lived with Grandma Loretta in her large farm house, a living arrangement that worked out for everyone. John and his grandmother were close and respected one another. Grandma Loretta helped with John's sons, and John made certain his grandmother was well cared for. Because John was involved in remodeling the old farm house, it was not in spotless condition. John seemed to be remodeling everything at once. But neither he nor Grandmother Loretta seemed to care.

Marcena and her husband (he was not involved in the fray) lived across the road in another farm house. Both Grandmother Loretta and John had difficulties with Marcena. She walked across the road several times a day to check on her mother. Although most of these visits were uneventful, sometimes Marcena would have what Grandmother Loretta described as a tantrum. Marcena would find something she disagreed with and give her mother a verbal tongue lashing. When John would find out about the criticism, he and his mother would have a major confrontation.

It was Marcena who arranged for the diagnostic sessions with the Alzheimer's Center. Everyone at the Alzheimer Center concluded that Grandmother Loretta had only slight signs of dementia. In reality she had a good mind for an eighty-three-year-old. I sat in on the second family conference during which Marcena and John took turns yelling at one another. Grandmother Loretta did not attend this conference. It upset her when her daughter and grandson became involved in one of their yelling matches.

Beneath all the strong words lay some obvious conclusions. Marcena honestly believed that her mother was living in an unsafe environment.

John encouraged his grandmother to live her life to the fullest, even if this might result in a fall or some other disaster. The antagonism between mother and son predated any disagreement over Grandmother Loretta's lifestyle.

I was given the assignment of dealing with the Winebergs. When I drove out to meet Grandma Loretta, I found her to be a delightful person. But she would not allow me to deal with her as the client, meaning that I would have deal with the family in three sessions. After meeting Grandma Loretta, I had three objectives, all of which would help the family get along better: I wanted to convince Marcena to tone down her criticisms; I wanted to encourage Grandma Loretta to continue to live independently, and I wanted to convince everyone to compromise a little.

Because of the depth of emotions in the family, I proposed an informal contract and asked each person to cooperate. I convinced Grandma Loretta to begin using a lifeline alert device, which she had always resisted, and become more tolerant of Marcena's concern. I asked John to become more cognizant of household safety. I pointed out to Marcena that the stressful situation was affecting her and affecting Grandma Loretta and that to some degree she had to let go. I was a bit devious: I indicated to John and Grandma Loretta that they were right and Marcena wrong, and that they should be more understanding of Marcena. I indicated to Marcena that John and Grandma were in the wrong and that she should be more understanding of them.

Admittedly, this was not a perfect approach; weekly sessions over a period of three months would have been preferable, but that was impossible.

I did the best I could in three sessions and it seemed to work. Every family member tried to compromise.

David

I received a call one day from Gary in California. His mother had died a week before, and Gary was concerned about his eighty-two-year-old father, David. "I'm afraid he's losing it. I believe we are talking about nursing home care." Gary described why he was concerned. His mother had been a difficult woman who had dominated his father. "When I returned for the first time in years," Gary said, "my parents' house was a disaster. Stacks of paper were everywhere, two-day-old food was laying around. My father seemed to have memory problems." When I asked about the relationship he had with his parents, Gary responded that "it was not good. We argued all the time. So finally I left."

Although I had some reservations about Gary's story, I went out to David's house expecting to find a small, wizened old man who could barely speak and who lived in a ramshackle house where he grieved for his deceased wife. Instead the house was situated in the old money section of town. When David opened the door, I was surprised to find an educated, cultured man.

The interior of the house was not spotlessly clean. Legal papers, bank records, and such were spread out on the dining room table. Perhaps half a dozen newspapers were stacked on a chair. I talked to David for an hour. He mentioned the disarray, saying "Excuse the mess. I'm sorting out our papers." Instead of a man enveloped in grief, I found a man going on with his life. Of course David was sad about his deceased wife, but he was considering visiting his brother in Michigan. He wondered about options for living. I described some retirement centers in the area but advised him against making any decisions for a few months.

Gary seemed disappointed that what I had found did not mesh with his opinion. After a few minutes, it became obvious that the son wanted an excuse to punish his father for whatever had happened between them. At the end of our conversation, I agreed to serve as his link to his father and to check on David every few months. Using the death of his mother as an excuse, I urged Gary to seek counseling.

Harley

Harley was a sixty-eight-year-old man who lived in an old mobile home in a rundown mobile home park. A couple watched over Harley because of a family connection, and they had purchased the used mobile home for Harley to live in. The couple had called the mental health center because Harley had related that sometimes he saw little people fighting on his bed.

Meeting Harley was quite an experience. He had grown up in Alabama and fathered ten children in Kentucky but didn't know where any of them lived. He had lived a marginal life: heavy drinking, day labor, and lots of women. Harley was a spinner of tall tales, and whenever I saw him he would tell me the same tall tales.

Harley talked freely of what he called his visions. "I just see 'em sometimes," he said. His life was predictable: when his Social Security check came in, he drank heavily for two weeks, and then when his money was mostly gone, he slacked off until the next check. We discussed Harley's case at the mental health center. By mutual agreement, we attributed Harley's visions to a lifetime of heavy drinking. I still see Harley every six weeks or so. He calls me his buddy and spends the next hour retelling the same tall tales. I listen and watch for symptoms that might indicate his condition is worsening.

Clara

Clara lived in a small town with her son Ben, whom she described as slow. They lived in the house she and her husband bought sixty-three years ago. Walking into her house was like re-entering 1930. The furniture, the decor, and even Clara herself in her high-necked dresses, were of that era. Clara's husband had died a decade ago. They had raised four children. Clara and Ben did not have much money, but they were content.

Clara had called a local social service agency because she wanted someone to talk to. When I walked into her house, she served coffee at her kitchen table and spent an hour describing an event that had happened seventy years ago and continued to trouble her.

When Clara was twelve, her mother, a small-town beauty, had run off with a gambler. Clara, her brothers, and their father continued their life as best they could. Six months later an uncle took Clara to a small city in the area. He had heard that Clara's mother and the gambler were staying at a hotel there. "We found them in the dining room," Clara related. "They were such a handsome couple. My mother was wearing a beautiful dress. The gambler was such a handsome man. I walked up to the table. They were getting ready to leave. When my mother saw me, she said, 'Hello' and then they left."

The gambler tired of Clara's mother and left her a year later. Clara's mother then returned to claim Clara and one brother before filing for divorce. "She didn't want my brother, Sam," Clara said. At the hearing, Clara's mother forced Clara to testify that her father was abusive.

For all the ensuing years, what had happened so affected Clara that she had never felt at peace. Now that she was in her eighties, and after having felt guilty for seventy years, she had to talk about what had happened.

Counseling Clara was one of the easiest things I've ever done. When I saw Clara, she was ready to talk, and after she had told her story she felt great relief. In the subsequent three sessions, I worked on the two feelings that haunted Clara, helping her realize that she was not responsible for what her mother had done, and that she had been coerced into talking against her father when she was twelve.

One more task remained. Clara wanted her four adult children to know what had happened and how it had affected her. With the exception of the son who lived with her, Clara's children were scattered over the country. So together we wrote a letter. Clara told me what she wanted to say. I wrote a rough draft, showed it to her, and made whatever changes she suggested before writing final draft. Clara signed all the letters. We mailed them and Clara closed a chapter that had troubled her for seventy years.

Valerie

Anyone who believes the myth that the sex drive vanishes at sixty should meet Valerie. Valerie's marriage, which lasted forty-seven years, ended with the death of her husband Bill. Although she was sixty-seven when Bill died, she was not ready for the rocking chair.

Bill had been pretty much an invalid for the last six years of his life. Because of his illness, Valerie's sex life had ended some time ago, although Valerie was a perky and very attractive woman. A few months after Bill's death she placed an advertisement in a personal column. One of the men who responded to her ad was a sixty-two-year-old charmer. From the beginning, Valerie and Tom had what might be described as good chemistry. But before long Valerie noticed a change in Tom. He stopped calling her, except when he wanted sex. Then, when she would tell him it was over, he would turn on the charm and keep her dangling. Then he began teasing her by talking of other women.

When Valerie was referred to me by another agency, she was close to being the proverbial basket case: she was nervous, not sleeping well, and frustrated. During our weekly sessions we began to discuss how Tom was manipulating her and discovered that Valerie had not completed the grieving process for her husband.

Valerie was a woman of considerable insight, but she was so smitten with Tom that she did not want to give him up. For the past nine months Valerie has called me every six weeks or so for a session. We discuss the negatives of the relationship. She agrees with me and understands that she should break it off completely, but other men bore her. She tries to back slowly away from Tom. Sometimes she avoids him for a week or two, but just when she believes she is ready to end it, he calls her and charms her.

Valerie understands all this. In fact, she has begun treating Tom somewhat shabbily. Although he dislikes this treatment, he calls often enough to keep Valerie interested. I have no doubt that in time she will end the relationship. She will eventually tire of the way he dangles other women before her, but it may require another year or so. Love can be as exhilarating and as devastating for people in their sixties as it can for people in their twenties.

Laura

When Laura moved into her high-rise, the manager saw in her an attractive, sixty-two-year-old divorcee. She seemed friendly if a bit of a loner. Then the manager noticed Laura would be absent for two or three days and that Laura was putting wine bottles in the trash.

Laura did not object to my seeing her. Neither did she deny that sometimes she drank too much. So we began our sessions rather conventionally, talking about parents who were not ideal and about her concerns for her four adult children. Although friendly, there was a sadness about Laura that I hoped was correctable.

Not long after our weekly sessions began, Laura spoke of swelling and pain in her stomach that increased in intensity. A month later she was brought to the hospital with cirrhosis of the liver. Only 5 percent of her liver was functioning. For the next several weeks no one knew if Laura would survive. Finally she improved to the point where her future looked bright and she returned home.

What was amazing was her spirit. The sadness had disappeared, and in its place was an ebullience, a sparkle that had not been there before. We talked about her change in attitude and personality. She had been so close to death that now she appreciated life for the first time in years. "I'm going to live every day," she said. "My liver could stop working at any time."

In Laura, I saw a typical example of how far motivation can take a person. Watching Laura change highlighted the truth that real change lies within the person. Counselors, psychiatrists, and psychologists can succeed only if the client allows that success.

Section Three

SOLUTIONS

Chapter 13

Making It Work

The preceding chapters have concentrated on two aspects of counseling third-age people: understanding the situations that make some people unusually vulnerable to the challenges of aging and providing suggestions for helping them cope with these situations. In this chapter, understanding and counseling are combined into an outline for action.

Past Dictates Present

Although you will encounter clients whose early years and adult lives have been models of stability, most of those who require assistance in dealing with the challenges of the third age will likely have had difficulty when they were younger. Instability may lurk beneath outward signs of success—declarations of a happy childhood, long-term marriage, and healthy children. Time and trauma may reveal subtle difficulties not immediately apparent. A predisposition toward anxiety or depression, an obsessive-compulsive tendency, emotional, physical, or sexual abuse by parent or spouse are some of the difficulties not obvious in initial sessions. To complicate matters, socially skillful people often try to cover concerns. While some clients will reveal their innermost concerns at the first session, other clients will make you dig for those concerns or difficulties.

Despite the degree to which the past determines the present and the need to deal with difficulties rooted in the past, counselors are not psychoanalysts. Not only are they not trained for twice weekly sessions last-

153

ing three years, they also lack the time to engage in such treatment. (Psychoanalysis remains a choice only for those who can afford the time and the $90 to $150 per session fee.) Many counselors on the other hand engage in brief therapy, lasting for one to a dozen sessions. It is important to understand how best to use these scant sessions, for you will be dealing with concerns that were a lifetime in the making.

When considering the difficulty of the task, it is courageous to even attempt to provide meaning and help to a troubled life in such a short time. And yet what you can accomplish in half a dozen sessions is amazing. By looking for hints of past problems and giving your client an opportunity to discuss and develop insight into troubled periods, you can help most clients develop a capacity to deal with present concerns.

If you recall, Clara had been just twelve years old when her mother ran off with a gambler. To make the situation worse, when her mother returned and filed for divorce against Clara's father, she forced Clara to testify falsely in court against her father. Seventy years passed during which Clara married a good man, raised four stable children, and lived an exemplary life. Yet throughout her life, Clara lived with the memory of what had happened. "I thought of it every day of my life," she said. The memories remained so potent because of guilt. Clara blamed herself for what her mother had done. As her counselor, I had to encourage Clara to talk about that painful time and help her understand that she was not responsible for what had happened. At eighty-two, Clara began to deal with her feelings. I remember sitting at Clara's table in her turn-of-the-century kitchen. As she unburdened herself, I was saddened by how Clara had lived so many years with such needless pain. After she finished her story, we talked about what had happened. For the first time, Clara understood that she had been only twelve years old and that she was not to blame for what her mother had done and forced her to do. After telling her story for the first time and understanding that she did not deserve the guilt that had plagued her, she felt tremendous relief. When I left, I hugged her. She was crying, but she said, "I feel so much better."

Actually, I had done very little. I had encouraged her to talk and had made some obvious observations. Although I saw Clara half a dozen times, I basically accomplished my goals in that first session.

Most symptoms of mild mental illness—anxiety, depression, panic attacks, and relationship problems, are symptoms of inner turmoil. This inner turmoil more than likely has been festering for years. Often the victim has dealt with this festering turmoil by ignoring it while going through the mechanics of living. When faced with the challenges of the third age, vulnerability surfaces and the façade crumbles.

Blanche typifies the individual who lives behind a façade much of her life only to succumb to the challenges of aging.

Blanche lived in a tiny cluttered garage apartment dominated by a large portrait of her father, a man who had dominated Blanche both before and after he died. She managed to live a reasonably normal life during her second age, marrying and raising two children while working in the family business. But then her husband died, and her health began to deteriorate. She had difficulties with her two adult children. This all happened within a few years, and Blanche could no longer live behind her façade. She could barely cope with the every-day demands of life.

Where Clara opened the door and worked hard with me in the counseling process, Blanche could only open the door part way. She refused to discuss how her father had affected her life. She ventilated and felt better because of it, but she went no farther. "My father always told me I should be strong," she said. Blanche continues to live a troubled life. I'll give her a couple of months and then call her. Maybe we can then complete what we started so Blanche can live in peace.

According to my theory of magnification of personality, who we are and what we feel during the first two-thirds of our lives becomes magnified in our third age. People who have had a happy childhood and a stable adult life not only deal positively with the challenges of the third age but also become stronger. Those whose past was difficult become more vulnerable and their instability becomes magnified. Blanche provides an example of this magnification of personality.

Another example can be found in Annette. She grew up with cold, critical parents and was twenty-eight when her mother died. On the day of the funeral, Annette's father told her that she and her brother were "foster children." "They didn't care enough about me to tell about it," she said. "I'm illegitimate." Annette brooded about this situation for forty years, living half a life. She married three times. Her relationship with her daughter was troubled. She refused to cooperate with mental health professionals who sought to help her. Her mental anguish only increased as she aged. When I tried to help her, she refused my help as well. She continues to live an unhappy life, focusing on her forty-year-old grievance against her long deceased parents.

Look for clues to past difficulties that account for your client's present weakness and limitations. Then look beyond these limitations and help your client recognize and build on his or her strengths. "You must be a strong person to have survived all that," I once told a client after she had related a story of abuse and devastation both in childhood and in marriage. The woman was amazed. "No one ever said that to me before. I've always thought of myself as weak. But you're right. I must be a strong person." Strength is what is perceived by the individual as strength. Clients who suddenly perceive themselves as being strong, can build upon that belief.

While the past usually determines the present, you will also encounter situations in which too much is demanded of an individual. Many people are strong enough to withstand one challenge. However, when fate asks them to deal simultaneously with several challenges, they may wilt under the pressure. In situations like this, don't become too concerned about the past; provide the support needed to help your client deal with the present.

Remain Flexible

While you look for clues about the past, remain flexible in forming judgments. Not long ago I had a conversation with a man who has spent many years in the mental health field and whose opinion I value greatly. "You know," he said, "I think seniors are the most difficult mental health population to work with. You never know whether the problems are mental or physical, side effects from medication, or some sort of dementia."

While making decisions concerning these areas, you must remain flexible and open to new information and facts which might lead you to consider other options.

Dorothy offers an example of why you must remain flexible.

If you recall, the manager of the high-rise where Dorothy lived called the mental health center crisis hotline because Dorothy was babbling incoherently. When the crisis worker went out to see her at midnight, he found a woman with numerous psychotic symptoms. When I visited her the next morning, I too saw a woman with psychotic symptoms. Then I learned that Dorothy had become upset about the Branch Davidian disaster in Waco and probably had not slept for three days. When I left at 9:30 a.m., I encouraged her sleep for several hours and told her that I would return at 3:30 p.m.

I spent half the intervening time trying to decide how to deal with Dorothy, who because of her religion would not accept either medication or hospitalization. That afternoon I returned to find her a reasonably rational woman. I was shocked. After seeing her a few times, I realized that Dorothy was a very fragile woman who would become obsessed with outside events, go days without sleep, and then behave irrationally. This event also taught me to remain flexible and avoid making judgments on initial evidence.

After counselors have worked in the field for awhile, there is a tendency to become smug about diagnostic abilities. Ninety-five percent of the time, your early diagnosis will be correct. But unique situations defy diagnostic logic. In unique situations the symptoms may only partially reflect the situation. Only after you get to know your client or have had a chance to talk with his or her family or friends can you be certain about your diagnosis. You must remain alert and flexible, and not make hasty diagnostic judgments.

When first meeting a client, you will make major decisions in four areas: diagnosis, past/present, approach, and resolution. You may have tentative thoughts about these four areas after the initial session, but you must remain flexible, staying open to further information in subsequent sessions.

Diagnostic Questions

Is the problem mental, medical, physical, or a combination of the three? If mental, is the depression, anxiety, or stressful response a situational reaction to a challenge? If medical, is the symptom a side effect of medication or perhaps the result of poor nutrition? If physical, are the symptoms the result of early dementia? Problems can arise, of course, from a combination of the above. In its earliest stage, dementia can masquerade as depression or anxiety, and Depression can masquerade as dementia. Diagnostic issues can prove puzzling.

Remain flexible, don't rush into a concrete, unshakable diagnosis that may have no relation to the true cause of a problem.

Past / Present

Remaining flexible is also important in discerning whether symptoms result from a current situation or from lifelong problems. Clients usually benefit from some discussion of troubled periods in their lives. This discussion usually provides some insight, and this may be the first step in dealing with current symptoms. But don't become too committed to dealing with the past when the client may be overwhelmed by situational problems in the present.

Approach the facts before making decisions about diagnosis and about past and present, before deciding on the best approach to use with your client. Is this an intensive counseling situation or would a problem-solving approach be more beneficial? Does your client have the capacity to develop insight into the situation? Should you nudge the client toward insight or assume a more directive role? Again, remain flexible before making a decision and stay open to shifting your approach through the counseling process.

Resolution

As you ponder diagnosis, the past and the present, and the approach to use, also consider what kind of resolution is possible. Is your client capable of substantive change, or will you simply help your client deal with the situational concern? Determine the goal of resolution before deciding on the approach. If anxiety is merely the result of a stressful situation, then you may opt for relaxation exercises. If the cause of the anxiety was instilled in your client forty years ago, then the past needs to be explored. In some situations, you may map out one approach only to find that your client is incapable of dealing with substance. This, of course, changes both the approach and the resolution.

Much of the time, you'll learn the answers to most of these questions within the first ten minutes you spend with a client. Other times several sessions may be necessary before answers are forthcoming. Even then you may not be certain as to diagnosis, past or present causes, approach, and resolution. In these more complex situations, the counselor must remain flexible throughout his or her work with the client.

Capacity for Change

One of the major myths about people over sixty is that they are too old to change. Nothing could be more inaccurate. An immense amount of change is required of people who are sixty-plus. Customarily, issues such as retirement adjustment, sickness, loss of loved ones, family problems, and economic problems must be dealt with. Frequently, third-age people must deal simultaneously with these and other concerns. They become very familiar with the requirements of change that accompany aging.

Compare the challenges of the third age with those at other stages of life, when challenges are generally faced one at a time. Recovering from the effects of a divorce may require an adjustment of two years for a forty-year-old, but compare this with the adjustment demanded of that forty-year-old's parent. During the same two year period, the parent may have dealt with retirement adjustment, loss of a spouse, economic problems due to living on a smaller income, and moving to another state.

Those who survive their sixth and seventh decade have dealt with considerable change. Regardless of the difficulty or combination of difficulties, many third-age people heartily accept fate-imposed change. Counselors never see the 80 percent who deal with the challenges of aging without outside help. They see the vulnerable 20 percent who ask for help. Everyone has a different capacity to deal with change.

If you recall, I cited three clients who had different capacities for change. Mary Ruth, who kept being evicted from high-rises because of her disagreeable personality, had no capacity or motivation to change. She would twist any comment into a personal affront and be on the attack believing that she was right and everyone else was wrong. There were reasons why Mary Ruth had such a disagreeable personality, but she would not permit an open discussion of her life. To make changes that would allow her to deal more effectively with the world would have required considerable introspection on her part, and Mary Ruth lacked the willingness to look at her life and embrace change.

Carl and David were both capable of change. Carl, whose wife was in a nursing home after a stroke, disliked his solitary life so much that he considered suicide. But when I pointed out that he could deal with his concerns and develop a new life, he vigorously embraced the possibility of change. David, the executive who was forced to retire, seemed unaware that his drinking was becoming a problem. After his wife became alarmed and sought help, he did not withdraw into drink; rather, he, like Carl, welcomed change and began using his considerable talents to help underprivileged youths.

Every client has a different capacity for change. With some clients, all you'll do is clarify the options, and your clients will make the change themselves. Other clients need to be nudged into believing that change is an option and then into making the necessary changes. Still other clients can change only enough to cope with a current concern. Most gratifying are clients such as Carl and David whose capacity for change allows them to develop new goals and build new lives.

Bear in mind these four thoughts:

1. The past dictates the present.
2. Always remain flexible and examine closely all factors contributing to symptoms.
3. Most clients have the capacity to deal with their situations.
4. You can usually deal with your clients' concerns within the parameters of brief therapy.

Now, serve your clients well, and protect the third age!

APPENDICES

Overview

These appendices consist of an elaboration of counseling techniques and aids that you might use with your clients; some principles of brief therapy; a brief discussion of psychiatric medications that psychiatrists or physicians might prescribe in specific situations; several relaxation aids; and a list of books for further reading.

Appendix 1. Assessment Aids

Appendix 2. The Initial Session

Appendix 3. Brief Therapy

Appendix 4. Cognitive Therapy Aids

Appendix 5. Helping Clients Understand Themselves

Appendix 6. Supportive Therapy Aids

Appendix 7. Relaxation Aids

Appendix 8. Psychiatric Medication Review

Appendix 9. Resource List

Appendix 1

Assessment Aid

E ach counselor develops a personal approach to assessment. Some employ a detailed assessment, while others use an informal method of assessment. I postpone the formal assessment until the second or third session. In the first session, I establish rapport by encouraging the client to discuss a concern.

This approach answers many questions normally involved in an assessment.

Here are general questions that might be asked in the initial counseling stages as assessment questions.

Intake Questions

When first interviewing a client, begin to gather information about the concern that has created your client's difficulties. Substitute, as appropriate, the specific concern.

How does the concern appear?

How often has the concern appeared?

How long has the concern existed?

How does the concern affect you?

How does the concern affect your thinking?

How does the concern affect your behavior?

Does the concern interfere with your life?

Does the concern surface when a specific situation exists?

Does the concern surface when around a specific person?

What happens before the concern appears?

What happens after the concern appears?

Personal / Family History

How would you describe your parents?

What kind of a relationship did they have?

How would you describe your brothers and sisters?

What kind of relationship do you have with them?

What kind of family life did you have when you were growing up?

How far did you go in school?

When did you get married?

How many times did you marry?

How would you describe your spouse(s)?

How many children did you have?

What kind of life do they lead now?

What is your relationship with your children/grandchildren?

How is your health?

Do you have major health problems now?

What medications are you taking now?

Anyone in your family have difficulty with drugs or alcohol?

What is your alcohol consumption?

How much coffee/tea/cola with caffeine do you drink a day?

Did you have a happy childhood?

How was alcohol used in your family?

Were you abused physically, sexually, or emotionally?

Lifestyle

(Here, you attempt to discover how your client lives.)

What is your typical day like?

How often do you leave your home?

What time do you get up in the morning?

What time do you go to bed in the evening?

What do you eat for breakfast, lunch, and dinner?

Do you go out with friends?

If you could make changes in the way you live, what changes would you make?

What kind of support system do you have?

Do you exercise regularly?

What kind of support services are you now receiving?

Has a social worker ever visited you?

Whether you conduct a formal or informal intake interview, you will be looking for clues. What clues do you receive from the client's physical appearance, dress, posture, gestures, facial expression, and voice quality? How does the client relate to you? What is the quality of his or her information, vocabulary, and thought processes? What is the emotional response? What about stream of thought, logic, and capacity to speak his or her mind? Throughout the intake process, attempt to decide what counseling approach to use with the client.

Appendix 2

The Initial Session

In the initial session with a client, you will be attempting to accomplish a number of goals. Whether you can accomplish all these goals depends on the client. Your client may be ready to share openly in the first session or may need two or three sessions to establish the rapport that allows comfortable sharing.

In the first session, attempt to cover the ten following elements.

1. Look for the problem.

If the client reports that he or she is depressed or nervous but will not elaborate, obviously this person is not sharing the whole story. Although your client can suffer from depression or anxiety without other symptoms, usually these symptoms appear because of underlying causes. Health problems, and especially pulmonary or respiratory difficulties, can produce anxiety. I once had the client who willingly discussed her depression, but it was not until the third session that she shared how distraught she was over her relationship with her daughter. While looking at symptoms you will be trying to discern what really brought the person to you.

2. Look for the attainable.

Counselors sometimes view themselves as miracle workers. Yet a client may have spent a lifetime developing relatively unresolvable conditions. Counselors who encounter this sort of client should seek attainable goals. Your client wants to see progress, and you want to help your client by facilitating progress. Together with your client, decide on initial attainable goals. Later in the counseling relationship, you may set more difficult goals.

3. Look for strengths and limitations.

All clients, despite their problems, have strengths, and from the first session seek to recognize strengths that can be built upon. Remember that the client who comes in for counseling often has been battered by circumstances, and may have forgotten about personal strengths. So you should look for strengths and help build on them.

Simultaneously, look for limitations so you can understand the capacity of your client. Sometimes a limitation such as extreme abuse in childhood overpowers strengths accumulated in a lifetime. Health limitations can be dealt with by focusing on strengths.

4. Look at the quality of social relationships.

Family relationships may constitute your client's strengths or limitations. If your client has a supportive adult child, this is a strength. Should your client have an abusive or demanding adult child then it is a limitation. Your client must succeed despite the relationship. Although the same might be said about friendships, they usually are a sign of strength rather than of limitation.

5. Look for a motivation that will insure success.

Sometimes you can work with two clients with similar concerns, and one will deal effectively with it, while the other makes little progress. In many situations, the difference between success and failure is the amount of motivation generated by a client. Although clients who are not motivated often achieve only moderate success in dealing with their concerns, clients who are highly motivated usually succeed.

6. Look for evidence of physical health.

Physical health often relates directly to concerns of third-age people. Not only does poor physical health affect mental health, poor physical health may also create concerns. An insecure person often has more difficulty dealing with poor physical health than a secure person. Physical problems magnify the concerns of third-age people.

7. Look at the physical environment.

Where and how your client lives provides considerable evidence about the background and self-image of your client. You can enter a dirty, unkempt apartment or house and see the home in two ways. If the dirtiness appears to be simply part of someone's lifestyle, so be it. If the dirtiness appears to be the result of lack of care, perhaps from depression or dementia, then the state of the home provides you with a major message.

8. Describe the therapy.

When you first see a third-age client, it may well be the first time this person has had counseling. Your client may have a warped concept of what takes place in a counseling session. The closest most people have been to counseling is watching a movie in which the client lies on a couch talking aimlessly while a pipe-smoking psychiatrist sits half asleep in chair. To ease your client's mind, provide a game plan at the end of a first session. Tell him or her how the counseling process works, the number of projected sessions, whether homework might be involved, and the degree of success client and counselor might expect to achieve.

9. Describe the process.

Always remember to be concrete. With the cooperation of the client, set an attainable goal and work toward it. It is important that a first-time client recognize that change and effective dealing with concerns is possible but that time and effort are required. I often compare working toward goals with climbing stairs. The counselor and client proceed forward a step at a time.

10. Describe the benefits of homework.

Not every counselor uses homework. Some clients seem almost incapable of working by themselves; others have difficulties for which homework is inappropriate. But for the right client with the right concern, homework can greatly improve both the final prognosis and the speed of recovery. A technique known as journaling is an example of homework that might prove beneficial. Encourage your client to keep a journal, to write down anything that comes to mind regarding the problem or concern. This journal is the private property of your client. During the sessions, encourage your client to read what he or she wants to share. This technique stimulates a client to record personal thoughts about a concern. By reading excerpts and working further with the material, your client enhances the counseling process.

During the first session, you will develop a sense of who the client is and what the client's concerns are, and you will also help the client understand what will happen in therapy sessions. When working with a third-age client, a counselor often plays a more active role and intercedes more *informally* than with other age groups. Your goal is to help your client understand and own the problem and develop new ways of thinking and dealing with the problem or concern.

Appendix 3

Brief Therapy

Yͭou will usually have between six to fourteen sessions with a client. When your client quits after one to three sessions, you may feel that you have failed.

However, when a client quits after a few sessions his or her desired goals may well have been accomplished. From my experience and that of others who have written about brief treatment, two elements dictate success in one-to-three session therapy: what kind of person is capable of change in a few sessions and what kind of change is achievable in this period?

Who Is a Candidate for Brief Therapy?

Before describing who might be a candidate for brief therapy, let's look at who is not a candidate for brief therapy. Clients who require more than three sessions include:

- People who have had a lifetime of problems, of living on the edge.
- People who may have physical or physiological problems, chemical imbalance, genetic tendencies, neurological problems, or brain damage.
- People who come to the first session prepared to return for an extended number of sessions.
- People who have chronic degeneration due to health problems.

These individuals would never be candidates for brief treatment. People with a lifetime of problems and those who have previously sought extended counseling sessions, come in not with one but with several problems. Dealing with a plethora of problems and/or satisfying the client in a short period of time is almost impossible.

Clients who are capable of achieving personal goals in a brief usually have one or more of the following characteristics:

- They are basically stable individuals concerned about a specific problem.
- They come in with an acute problem rather than with a long-term condition.
- They need confirmation that their problem is insoluble, that they must live with their problem.
- They may be obsessed or stuck in a process because of a past event and want to resume a more normal lifestyle.

What Goals Are Achievable in Brief Therapy

A client whose needs might be met in one or two sessions comes in with a specific question: How can I deal with this problem? Is what I am feeling a normal feeling? How can I get over the death of my spouse? Is there any way I can stop feeling depressed, angry or anxious? When your client finds an answer to his or her specific question and understands the situation, there may be immediate relief from the pressure. While some clients want to continue counseling to fully work through their concerns, other clients want to quit immediately. Usually clients who have had their questions answered have no interest in continuing counseling.

Clients whose needs are met with brief therapy are clients whose concerns are solvable. They need permission to grieve, to dislike, to be angry, or to feel. Or they need to understand that they are not guilty, that whatever happened was not their fault. Some clients may need another's opinion or permission to fully experience their emotions. Clients whose needs can be met with brief therapy are ready to deal with their concerns but simply require a nudge or two.

Appendix 4

Cognitive Therapy Aids

Cognitive therapy was developed by Albert Ellis and others as rational-emotive therapy. Working with this model, the counselor assumes that thoughts cause feelings. It is not events or people that upset us but our personal beliefs about ourselves. Negative self talk is allowed to affect our mindsets and create concerns and problems. Although everyone is subject to negative thinking from time to time, some people develop serious patterns of negative thinking. Counselors can use cognitive strategies to assist those troubled by negative thinking patterns.

Three Situations That May Lead to Negative Thinking

When one of more of these situations recur several times, negative feelings about one's competence and sense of mastery may develop:

1. Things happen that he/she believes shouldn't happen.

A divorced woman in her fifties attends a party. Men have always approached her in these situations but now none do and she makes no attempt to approach them. She leaves the party convinced that all the stories she's heard are true: "Once you pass fifty, all the men are looking for younger women. No man will ever want to talk to or date me." Actually, she might have said to herself, "I am an attractive, intelligent woman. I will have an opportunity to meet a man who will appreciate me."

2. Thinking or behavior about others becomes extraordinarily negative.

It is easy to fall into the trap of thinking negatively or cynically about people. After a series of disenchanting experiences, a person may maintain that "you cannot trust anyone." Then the person avoids people because of this feeling of distrust. Although the world has its share of people who will lie and cheat, the world has far more people who will return warmth and support in exchange for honesty and fair treatment. The cynical person might instead have said, "I will be more selective about friends and confidants."

3. He/she always reacts the same way during times of crisis.

It's only natural that people react in the same way to *similar* events and *similar* sources of stress. However, crises often mark turning points in people's lives. A crisis might mark the time when a person should begin considering different options. I once knew a man who throughout his life would start drinking heavily when faced with a difficult situation. Every time he faced a difficult situation, he dwelt on negative thoughts and convinced himself he could not deal with that situation. In effect, he dealt with the difficult situation by avoiding it through intoxication.

The ABC Model

Albert Ellis describes the thinking process in what he calls the A-B-C Model. A is an activating event, B is a person's thinking about that event, and C represents subsequent feelings and behaviors.

Example of The A-B-C Model:

A) Activating Event: (Mary's spouse dies)

B) Mary's Thinking: (I am a forty-seven-year-old widow. John did everything for me. I'm nothing without him. My life is over.)

C) Feelings and Behaviors: In addition to her normal feelings of grief, Mary begins a new life convinced of her incompetence without her husband. She feels this way and so lives her life this way.

Mary is preparing to live a life based on a faulty assumption. Granted, she is now a widow; however, John did not do everything for her. Although she will miss him and her life will change, she is a capable human being who can create a new life. People aware of their faulty reasoning can use the A-B-C Method to dispute irrational thinking. After A happens, they can challenge B (their thinking). After challenging their thinking, they can choose different ways of behaving and reacting to the precipitating event.

Thought Stopping

A slightly different way of refuting irrational thoughts is a technique called thought stopping. With the A-B-C Method the content of one's thoughts is analyzed; thought stopping involves attending to unwanted thoughts and purging one's mind of these thoughts. This technique is effective with sexual preoccupation, obsessive thoughts of failure and inadequacies, and obsessive memories. It works this way: stressful thoughts are listed, then imagined; when that thought appears, one yells either aloud or silently; finally appropriate thought is substituted for stressful thought.

With cognitive strategies, a person seeks to overcome negative, problem-creating, self talk and substitute in its place positive self talk. Positive self talk provides a more accurate, healthier view of reality and enhances coping skills in stressful situations.

Common Distortions

When people have negative views of themselves, they often view the world from a distorted perspective. The distortions can be minor ones that create little more than discomfort; other distortions grossly warp one's perspective of the world. Here are some examples of how people can distort their image of themselves:

Overgeneralization

People who overgeneralize actually look for an excuse for self-condemnation. They might think, "I always screw up. No matter what I do, I fail." When they make a mistake they consider this mistake an example of their constant failure.

Filtering

People who filter reality sift through a situation seeking an indication that matches an ingrained belief. During a conversation, for example, they may look for a critical comment. Hearing four positive comments and one negative comment they will ignore the positive comments and remember only the negative one.

Self blame

People who engage in self blame always blame themselves for every negative happening, whether or not that blame is deserved. Self-blaming people blame themselves for being imperfect. Lacking an innate skill in mathematics, they will blame themselves for being stupid. They will blame themselves for aspects of life only marginally within their control.

Control fallacies

Some people seek to control every aspect of life. When they are not in control, they feel helpless and vulnerable. "Control freaks" believe it is important to influence and to control other people. By doing so, they avoid the overwhelming feelings that surface when they lack control.

Mind reading

Mind readers assume that all people think alike, and possess the same view of the world that they do. A mind-reading woman may believe she is too thin. When she notices someone looking at her, she will assume that person is thinking: "That woman is so thin. She looks so terrible." Because mind readers always assume the worst, they always assume other people are thinking negative thoughts.

Co-dependency

"Rescuers" can become so involved in someone else's problems or addictions that they lose sight of themselves. Women in our society are especially subject to tendencies of co-dependency. In traditional marriages a wife may base her life completely on being Mrs. So-and-So and have no identity outside her marriage. Parents may become so wrapped up in their children that they have no identity apart from them. A spouse may live with an alcoholic, and be so involved in that addiction that the lives of both spouse and the addicted person revolve around the addiction.

Many people suffer from some of the problems and irrationalities described above, but not to the same degree. An insecure person with low self-esteem may be overwhelmed by his or her irrationalities. Bullies have, in reality, low self-esteem and try to convince themselves by their actions that they are okay. Bullies often suffer from a combination of distortions, specifically control and mind reading. By threatening and controlling people, they assume other people are impressed by their behavior. Secure people simply deal with the irrationalities and distortions that overwhelm others.

Negative Mind Sets

From distorted thinking processes come a plethora of mindsets that affect how a person views and relates to the world. Some examples of negative mindsets include these verbalizations:

"I will be happy when…"

Some people spend their lives postponing happiness. They believe that when they reach a certain point in life, they will be happy—when the kids are grown, when they retire to Florida, when they have a grandchild, etc. Never happy in the moment, they always postpone fulfillment.

The mindset often results from looking outside rather than within for fulfillment. An example is the person who wants to marry the perfect mate, one who will provide total satisfaction.

"People must approve of me and my actions."

Some people live their lives pleasing others. They trade actions for approval. Anyone who constantly seeks approval and gratification from others loses any semblance of individuality. Pleasers often have difficulty adjusting to the challenges of the frail years. They have difficulty living alone, without having people to please. They really have no sense of inner self or inner strength. They must obtain validation from others.

"I am entitled to a life free of pain."

Part of the human experience consists of experiencing pain. An inability to cope with pain does not bode well for a person entering the frail years. The spirit needed to adjust and adapt to adversity is missing. Such a person more than likely has a master plan, and when this master plan does not work out, depression may set in.

"I am disappointed when I look in the mirror."

Through much of life, people are disappointed with how they look: they're too short or too tall, too fat or too thin. People can be disappointed with the facial features given to them by fate. Several studies have found that both men and women begin dealing with and accepting their physical image while in their fifties. Research also indicates that exceptionally attractive women have difficulty dealing with the physical changes accompanying aging. Some have used their features as a crutch and believe their success in life resulted from physical beauty rather than individual talent.

"Achievement and production determines my worth as an individual."

This attitude drives many people to accumulate prestige and money. Upon entering their third age, they find the prestige from the working years has lost its impact. Prior to entering the third age, they identified themselves through their occupation; upon retirement, this identification disappears and becomes relatively unimportant to most people. The third age is a great leveler—what matters most in your third age is not achievement and production but what you are as a person.

"I hate to be alone. Happiness, fulfillment, and pleasure come from being with others.

A person who constantly needs people often has difficulty adjusting to the third age. Spending time alone usually accompanies aging, and anyone who cannot deal with solitary living will probably experience unhappiness.

Appendix 5

Helping Clients Understand Themselves

Counselors often encounter clients who do not understand or accept themselves. Because of low self-esteem, a client may ignore strengths and focus only on limitations. Here are two aids to give to such clients as homework. The purpose of these exercises is to help these clients understand themselves and to recognize strengths that they may have overlooked.

A client who feels change is impossible may say, "Well, that's the way I am," and continue with life even though change is necessary. The purpose of the introspection promoted by these questions is to understand the forces that created the person and to understand that change is possible.

Who am I?

As you answer this question, try to describe to yourself who you are. Its purpose is to help you gain some personal insight into what happened in your life to make you who you are. To aid in this exercise of introspection, I'd like you to write an autobiography composed of the significant events in your life. I'd also like you to prepare a self-concept inventory.

The Autobiography

Beginning with your first memories, describe your life. The length of your autobiography is unimportant. Some people who have little propensity for writing may summarize their lives in a page. A more introspective person may require fifty pages. Using paper and pencil, a tape recorder, describe your life.

The Significant Event Autobiography

In this type of autobiography the focus is on the significant events, periods, or insights that occurred in your life. We all experience significant benchmark happenings that affect our lives. We lose or gain a friend, we lose a parent. Other examples might involve a sibling, meeting your spouse, or the birth of a child. Begin chronologically and describe in order the significant events in your life. This will help you gain insight into yourself and your life.

The Self-Concept Inventory

Using words or phrases, describe yourself in the following areas:

A. Physical Appearance

Describe your height, weight, facial appearance, skin, hair, style of dress—anything that describes the physical you. For example:

Large blue eyes

Olive complexion

Chubby thighs

Medium-sized breasts

Use little make-up

Like casual dress

Light brown hair

Clear skin

Slightly protruding teeth

Slightly hooked nose

Attractive when dressed up

Prefer jeans and T-shirt

B. Your Relationship to Others

Describe your strengths and limitations in relating to others—friends, family, co-workers, or strangers at a social setting such as a cocktail party. For example:

Flexible

Warm

Open

Difficulty saying no

Feel phony at parties

Too accepting

Too resentful when wronged

Compromise too quickly

Too accepting of strangers

Afraid to say what I think

Good listener

Socially competent but nervous

C. Personality

Describe your positive and negative personality traits. For example:

Responsible

Talk too much when nervous

Shy, try to be outgoing

Feel insecure when alone

Try too often to please

Like being busy

Pout sometimes

D. How Others Probably See You

Describe your strengths and limitations the way others may see you. For example:

Generally competent

Wishy-washy

Try to do too much

Dependable

Too dependent on others

Little scatterbrained

Smile too much

Can be controlled

E. How You Perform on the Job

Describe your general approach to work. For example:
Industrious, prompt

Try to be liked

Like to help people

Sometimes take on too much

Good at paperwork

F. How You Perform Daily Tasks

Describe how you manage in the little tasks of living. For example:
Keep appointments

Do too many things

Superficial housekeeper

Sometimes dress sloppily

Buy things I don't need

So busy that I eat poorly

G. How Your Mind Works

Describe how effective you are at problem solving, your capacity for creativity and learning, and your insights. For example:
Not good at challenging

Interested in people

Kind of a slow mind

Lost in intellectual discussions

Unaware what's happening in the world

Not very creative

After completing your self-concept inventory, mark a plus by traits or habits that you consider strengths and a minus by traits or habits you consider limitations.

What do you dislike about yourself?

Everyone has strengths and limitations. Sometimes people tend to focus on limitations and ignore strengths. How you feel about yourself affects what you consider strengths and limitations.

Answering this question requires focusing on limitations. Using your answers and your introspection from the first question make a list of things about yourself that you dislike. Include almost anything about you and your life that you dislike. For example:

My physical appearance

My personality

How I relate to others

How I feel about myself

How I treat myself

How I treat others

How others treat me

My personality, personality traits

How others look at me

How my mind works

How I handle the small, daily tasks of life

What do you like about yourself?

People often become so preoccupied with their gripes about themselves that they forget their strengths. Using as much honesty and detail as in listing your limitations, write about your strengths, about what you like about yourself. Use the same examples, or others, that you wrote about in your dislikes. Include what you consider your strengths in:

Your physical appearance

Your lifestyle

Your personality

How you feel about yourself

How you treat yourself

How you treat others

How others treat you

How others look at you

How your mind works

How you handle the small, dally tasks of life

How you handle major issues, major questions, major problems.

Anything else that you may think of that you like about yourself or about your life.

Personal Inventory

The previous three questions have been general. Now it is time to get specific. Take a few minutes to respond to this personal inventory and find out what kind of person you would like to become.

1. List your five major concerns and number them according to priority (1 = area of greatest concern): _____

_____

_____

_____

_____

2. List five habits that affect your life negatively (1 = most negative habit): _____

_____

_____

_____

_____

3. List five major sources of stress in your life (1 = greatest source of stress): _____

_____

_____

_____

_____

4. Evaluate three of your limitations as to cause, effect and consequences: _____

_____

_____

_____

_____

5. Necessary steps to overcome these limitations:_____

_____

_____

_____

_____

Search for a silver lining in your concerns. For example:

Concern: I am fat and breathe heavily when I walk.

Silver Lining: But I can shape up.

Concern: _____

Silver Lining: _____

Concern: _____

Silver Lining: _____

Concern: _____

Silver Lining: _____

Concern: _____

Silver Lining: _____

List four of your goals and the steps necessary to accomplish them:

Goal 1

Objective A: _____

Objective B: _____

Objective C: _____

Goal 2

Objective A: _____

Objective B: _____

Objective C: _____

Goal 3

Objective A: _____

Objective B: _____

Objective C: _____

Goal 4

Objective A:_____

Objective B: _____

Objective C: _____

Interpreting Inventory Lists

After completing your lists, put them away for a week. Then, after a week, examine each list carefully. Look for patterns and for evidence that describes you as a person. After examining these lists carefully, make a final list. In this final list, answer these questions:

1. What are my strengths as a person? _____

_____

_____

2. What are my limitations as a person?_____

_____

_____

3. What options are open to me to change or to cope with life?_____

_____

_____

As you review your lists and interpretations, you will likely discover that you have far more strengths and positive elements about your life than you previously thought. Remember, when you go through a difficult period of life, you may tend to look at life through darker glasses. However, when your life straightens out, you will find that your world is much brighter than you once thought.

The purpose of the foregoing activities is to help your client attain a greater level of understanding and acceptance. With more understanding, your client can recognize his or her strengths, which will help your client cope with difficulties. When people are overwhelmed with anxiety or depression, they tend to degrade themselves and to focus on limitations. Focusing on strengths can change this mindset.

Appendix 6

Supportive Therapy Aids

Supportive therapy consists of two elements: humanistic counseling and problem solving.

Humanistic Counseling

Advocates of humanistic counseling, psychology, and philosophy attribute noble qualities to the individual. Where others view people as irrational, unsocialized, and destructive, humanists view people as rational, socialized, and realistic. When a humanistic counselor observes jealousy, hostility, and viciousness in a client, that counselor, believing in the basic goodness of human nature, searches for an explanation for the inhumane thinking and then attempts to correct it. The explanation often reveals that the client has been the victim of inhumane treatment by others. The goal then becomes to undo the inhumane treatment.

In dealing with clients, a humanistic counselor observes these tenets:

People are basically good. Our innate nature is to treat people as if we are all good. People have a strong need for positive regard: we want other people to like us and respect us. Our high self regard leads us to like ourselves and consider ourselves as worthy.

Experiences sometimes undermine people's feelings for themselves, and they experience what humanistic writers describe as incongruence between the self and experience. This incongruence occurs when a discrepancy exists between the perceived self and the experience. The result is internal tension. (For example, a person spends a lifetime as a valuable, productive member of society and is treated by others as such. However, when this person reaches seventy years, he or she becomes the victim of ageism by either society or family. This maltreatment can result in anxiety, depression, or anger.)

A counselor can help the client return to a state of congruence by restoring confidence and a feeling of positive regard. The counselor uses all the following techniques to help the client achieve congruence: acceptance of the individual without question, unconditional positive regard for the client regardless of what the client says or does, and an empathic understanding of what the client feels. The counselor who uses client-centered therapy encourages the client to identify these feelings, to express how he or she feels, and either to alter or accept these feelings.

Perhaps the key to client-centered therapy is to identify and encourage the expression of emotions. The counselor picks up on cue words that indicate what the client is feeling. What follows are lists of cue words that fit into four classifications of feelings: affection, anger, fear, and sadness. A counselor who is alert to the expression of emotions, and to the cue words that point to emotions, can help his or her client recognize, acknowledge, and express a full range of feelings.

Cue Words of Anger

against	attack	angry	compete
argue	criticize	dislike	fight
hate	hit	hurt	nasty

Cue Words of Fear

anxious	awful	bothers	concerns
confused	cop out	dismay	doubt
failure	flunk	freak out	quarrel
protect	reject	resent	surly
neglect	run	from	scare
sneak	stuck	stupid	struggle
suffer	torn	between	

Cue Words of Sadness

abandoned	gloomy	adrift	grieve
alone	heartsick	depressed	isolated
disillusioned	listless	distressed	miss
missing	discouraged	sorrowful	despondent

Cue words of affection or regard

able	beautiful	can	cheerful
close	content	delighted	enjoy
excited	friendly	fulfill	great
happy	like	nice	optimistic
optimism	pretty	satisfy	smart
thrill	try	terrific	want
wish	worth		

After helping the client identify and express feelings, the next step is to alter or accept these feelings. I once worked with a woman whose father had abused her emotionally, physically, and sexually almost half a century ago. This experience had led to a lifetime of problems. Much of the woman's unhappiness resulted from suppressing her feelings and not dealing with them. Once I gave her permission to be angry with her father, who now suffered from Alzheimer's disease, my client became much more stable. When we explored the bizarre upbringing that probably accounted for her father's abuse, the woman altered her feelings toward her father. After understanding the concept of generation repetition, my client understood her own pain and her father's pain. She then was able to provide the support that he needed.

Problem Solving Support

When I started counseling third-age people, I questioned whether I could work effectively with clients whose office appointments were prearranged. It's not that this approach is bad, but the office approach doesn't work with some clients. With others, the counselor can best help the client by using the problem solving aspect of supportive therapy. Problem solving can be used on both major and minor problems, and often involves going out into the client's world to help solve the problems of real life.

Major problems are those concerns that interfere with the client's emotional health. Several times I have encountered clients who were estranged from their adult children. This estrangement was often caused by an in-law or by miscommunication. By acting as a mediator and clarifying the situation, I was able to eliminate a major source of stress and symptoms of anxiety and/or depression. The relationships did not immediately become perfect, but after a few sessions family members were talking to one another.

Minor problems are situations that cause discomfort. A client who once received a $636 bill from the hospital, paid in part by Medicare, was refused payment by supplemental insurance. The insurance firm was a reputable company, but it would not pay its twenty percent. When billed by the hospital, the company kept insisting that my client did not have a policy with them. One five-minute telephone call resolved the situation. It seems that a hospital computer operator had transposed two numbers of my client's insurance account, resulting in the insurance computer notifying the hospital computer that my client had no policy. Once the correct account number was entered, the matter was resolved, the bill was paid and my client slept well for the first time in several weeks.

When I recommend problem solving as a viable approach, I refer not to performing menial tasks for the client but to engaging in strategic intervention. A counselor can accomplish a lot with a telephone call, or a home visit. In this situation, a counselor can accomplish more in thirty minutes of problem solving than in half a dozen sessions of conventional counseling.

Humanistic counseling and problem solving mesh perfectly to produce supportive therapy. They mesh so perfectly because problem solving is simply a concrete way of showing the client the tenets of humanistic counseling. By intervening to straighten out a bill that is creating anxiety for a client, a counselor demonstrates that the client is valued and that the counselor is doing everything possible to provide relief. Not all clients require additional intervention. For those who do, though, the pragmatic approach of problem solving is an important element in the counseling process.

Appendix 7

Relaxation Aids

R elaxation aids are a means of helping the client relax and deal with pressures. When pressures tax the body, muscles tense, heart and respiratory rates increase, and many other changes occur. Relaxation aids also empower third-age clients; they gain a sense of control that may have been absent. There are many more relaxation aids than the four mentioned here: breathing exercises, physical exercise, meditation, and progressive muscle relaxation.

Western medicine has only recently become aware of the importance of breathing correctly. In the East, deep-breathing techniques have long been associated with mental, physical, and spiritual development. Here is one of many breathing exercises:

Breathing Awareness

Lie on the floor in a "dead body" pose: legs straight and slightly apart, toes pointed comfortably outward, arms at sides not touching the body, palms up and eyes closed.

Notice your breathing. Place your hands on the spot that rises and falls most as you inhale and exhale. If this spot is in your chest, you are not using the lower part of your lungs.

Place both hands on your abdomen and follow your breathing.

Breathe through your nose.

Move your chest in harmony with your abdomen.

Scan your body for tension, especially your throat, chest, and abdomen.

Practice deep breathing five or ten minutes at a time, once or twice a day. Slowly extend this period to twenty minutes.

When you have learned to relax by deep breathing, practice it when you feel yourself becoming tense.

Physical Exercise

Exercise is known to be valuable to the body, but we don't often hear of its value for the mind. Clients suffering from anxiety or depression are often possessed by negative feelings of helplessness or powerlessness. A regular exercise program contributes to dealing with negative feelings and to maintaining a positive, stable attitude after clients return to normality.

Dr. Joel Posner, medical director of the Philadelphia Geriatric Center, is halfway through a ten-year study of exercise and aging. Participants in the study consist of 400 people from sixty to a hundred years of age, and Dr. Posner has tentatively concluded that after six months of exercise a healthy participant may retain or regain physical capacity he or she possessed two to three decades earlier. A trained eighty-year-old can be in better shape than an untrained forty-year-old; people who have never exercised but who are not severely limited by disease can become fit by exercising properly; and much of what is considered decline due to age is really a decline resulting from disuse.

In another study, psychologist Alan A. Hartley of Scripps College in California has completed a study that links exercise and the mental ability of people from their mid-fifties on. He found that the more people exercised, the better their performance on reasoning, memory, and reaction-time tests. Differences between those who lived sedentary lives and those who exercised at least thirty minutes a day were significant, and when all others variables were taken into account—health, age, education, and vocabulary—the gap between those who exercised and those who did not exercise remained significant. Although there is much we don't know about why exercise stimulates the brain, more than likely both body and mind are involved. When a person exercises, more oxygen flows into an aging brain, enhancing one's mental functioning.

Exercising regularly provides these major benefits for third-age people:

- Exercise maintains physical health and wards off disease.

- Exercise permits a person to live a lifestyle of someone years younger.

- Exercise provides a feeling of control and well being.

- A person who begins and continues an exercise program proves that "I am a strong person."

- Exercise helps fight the blues by triggering a release of hormones that enhances a feeling of strength and wellness.

A psychiatrist who has seen many clients over the years once observed that, "I've never seen a physically fit depressed person."

An exercise program, whether formal or informal, should include aerobic exercise and strength exercise. Although jogging, skipping rope, and swimming are great exercises, most third-age people engage in walking. A good walking program burns almost as many calories as jogging, increases metabolism, helps curb appetite, reduces caloric consumption, and allows people of any age to participate. But everyone also needs some sort of strength-enhancing exercise, whether that exercise includes hefting a set of $10 dumbbells or using sophisticated machines at a health club. A person who engages in aerobic and strength-enhancing exercises enhances not only the body but also the mind and the general sense of well-being.

Mantra Meditation

Meditation creates a state of deep relaxation in a short time by decreasing metabolism, oxygen consumption, carbon dioxide production, respiratory rate, heart rate, and blood pressure. Meditation requires a quiet place, a comfortable physical position, an object or a word to dwell upon, and a passive attitude. There are many meditation exercises, among which the focusing of attention on a sound or sounds is quite popular.

A mantra is a meaningful or meaningless sound of two or more syllables repeated over and over incessantly in order to free the mind of other thoughts. A typical eastern mantra might be: *so-ham* (I am he) or *sa-ham* (I am she). Choose a mantra you feel comfortable with or request one from your teacher or counselor.

Find a quiet place and chant the mantra aloud. Let the mantra find its own rhythm as the sound of your voice helps you relax.

After chanting the mantra aloud for five minutes, whisper it, flowing into a deeper relaxation with the rhythm of the sound.

Chant fifteen minutes a day, five to seven days a week for two weeks, increasing the length of the session to thirty minutes. Whenever thoughts of the mundane world intrude, revert to vocalizing the words.

Progressive Muscle Relaxation

Sometimes called deep muscle relaxation, progressive muscle relaxation is based on the premise that the body responds to anxiety-provoking thoughts with muscle tension. The physiological tension increases anxiety. Deep muscle relaxation reduces physiological tension and as a result reduces anxiety.

From a comfortable position, either lying down or in a chair with head support, curl both fists and tighten biceps and forearms. Hold the position for five to ten seconds. Then relax for twenty to thirty seconds.

Wrinkle the forehead while pressing the head back as far as possible. Now wrinkle the muscles of the face, squint the eyes, purse the lips, and press the tongue against the roof of the mouth. Hunch the shoulders, hold the position for five to ten seconds, then relax.

Arch back while taking a deep breath. Hold, then relax. Take a deep breath, pressing out the stomach. Hold and then relax. Pull the feet and toes back toward face while tightening the shins. Hold, then relax. Curl the toes while tightening the calves, thighs, and buttocks. Hold and relax.

There are many ways of relaxing. What works for one person may not work for someone else. The methods described above are simply methods of relaxation that have worked for many people over the years.

Appendix 8

Psychiatric Medication Review

M ost counselors, social workers, and psychologists complete their education without learning much about medication. Learning about uses, dosages, and specific medications occurs on the job. Because the world of psychiatric medication changes so rapidly, some medications on this list will fall out of favor while new medications will appear.

Psychiatric Medications and Third-Age People

The purpose of psychiatric medication is to diminish the symptoms that upset clients. Three types of medications are often prescribed for third-age people: anti-anxiety, antidepressant, and antipsychotic medications. While anti-anxiety medications are prescribed to reduce anxiety and antidepressants are prescribed to deal with depression, antipsychotic drugs are used for slightly different situations in treating late onset mental illness. Antipsychotic drugs have been prescribed primarily in cases of late onset paranoia and Alzheimer's victims who exhibit serious behavioral problems.

Psychiatric medications should be dispensed to third-age clients with caution. Some medications produce side effects such as dizziness, confusion, unsteadiness, and memory loss, and may be harmful for third-age clients.

Some medications involve risks such as addiction, paradoxical reaction, and tardive dyskinesia. Correct dosage is as important as selection of medication; overmedication can result in some of the serious side effects mentioned above. Third-age people are generally more sensitive to medication than other age groups.

Individual differences are also extremely important. Randomly chosen seventy-year-olds include several different physical types, some unhealthy and frail with a body in the final stages of deterioration, others healthy, physically fit, more like fifty-year-olds than seventy-year-olds; the rest somewhere between the two extremes. Competent psychiatrists and physicians consider a client's physical condition as well as state of mind when prescribing a drug and dosage. Since many individuals in this age population are already taking other medications for physical health problems, the physician must consider the possibility of problematic drug interactions.

Another concern involves correct ingestion of the drugs. Most clients on psychiatric medication follow instructions to the letter, taking the medication as prescribed, but some have had great difficulty in taking medication as prescribed. An Alzheimer's victim may no longer possess the cognitive skills necessary to take medication properly. Sadly enough, in many cases, the more important the medication is to the client, the greater the possibility of taking the medication improperly. The help of family or friends is invaluable in such cases.

The cost of medication poses another problem. Many clients live on $400 to $700 Social Security checks and must also pay for medication for physical problems. When asked to pay for psychiatric medication, they must scrimp even more or forsake the medication because of cost.

Family Physicians

Family physicians prescribe the bulk of antidepressants and anti-anxiety medications for third-age people. People go to their friendly family physician when they have a problem. They may have a fear of psychiatrists and of being thought mentally unsound, so they prefer to deal with their family physician even when the problem is mental. And yet every counselor, social worker, and psychologist would prefer that their depressed or anxious client see a psychiatrist, who can make a diagnosis from the symptoms, and then prescribe a medication that best fits the situation.

Psychiatrists specialize in psychiatric medication. While family physicians may make reasonably decent judgments in prescribing antidepressants and anti-anxiety medications, they do not know all the nuances of psychiatric medication. Many family physicians will shy away from prescribing antipsychotic medication and are not aware that some antidepressants do not work effectively with third-age people. Some family physicians err in prescribing dosages and in expecting one medication to deal with certain symptoms; a psychiatrist may see the need for a combination of two medications to deal with a complex problem. For these reasons, most counselors prefer that their clients receive psychiatric medications from psychiatrists. Psychiatrists are not perfect, but on the whole they are far more proficient than family physicians at making diagnoses and prescribing medications for psychiatric problems, especially when the problems are complex and multi-faceted. I counseled a woman once who suffered from a mix of Alzheimer's disease, major depression, and organic brain deterioration. Over a period of several years she saw five psychiatrists: the result was five different diagnoses and five different prescriptions of medications. Nothing worked. The woman today remains in a nursing home and displays the same complex symptoms as when I first saw her.

Nowadays, most psychiatrists evaluate clients, make diagnoses, and dispense psychiatric medications. They rarely provide counseling to third-age clients. The ideal psychiatrist gathers information by listening to the client, the counselor, and the family before prescribing a medication. If the medication does not seem to work, then the psychiatrist adjusts either the dosage or the medication itself.

Anti-Anxiety Medications

Most anti-anxiety medications take effect quickly, providing relief in minutes to hours. Because this group of medications has addictive qualities, most are designed not to be taken for more than thirty days, though some clients with major anxiety problems take various medications of this sort for far longer periods. Some commonly prescribed anti-anxiety medications are listed on the next page under their brand names and generic names.

Brand Name	Generic Name
ATIVAN, LOPRAZ, ALZAPAM	lorazepam
BUSPAR	buspirone
CATAPRES	clonidine
INDERAL	propranolol
PAXIPAM	halazepam
SEREX	oxazepam
TRANXENE	chlorazepate
XANAX	alprazolam

Antidepressants

While most anti-anxiety medications become effective in minutes to hours, antidepressants respond more slowly. It may take two to four weeks to provide relief. Antidepressants do not have the same addictive qualities as anti-anxiety medications, and people can take antidepressants for years without becoming addicted. Some commonly prescribed antidepressant medications are:

Brand Name	Generic Name
ASENDIN	amoxapine
ANAFRANIL	clomipramine
DESYREL	trazodone
ELAVIL, ENDEP, EMITRIP, AMITRIL	amitriptyline
EUTONYL	pargyline
LUDIOMIL	maprotiline
MARPLAN	isocarboxazid
NARDIL	phenelzine
NORPRAMIN, PERTOFRANE	desipramine
PAMELOR, AVENTYL	nortriptyline
PARNATE	tranylcypromine
PROZAC	fluoxetine
SINEQUAN, ADAPIN	doxepin
SURMONTIL	trimipramine
TOFRANIL, TOFRANIL-PM, JANIMINE, TIPRAMINE	imipramine
VIVACTIL, NEOACTIL	protriptyline
WELLBUTRIN	bupropion HCl

197

Antipsychotic

Antipsychotic medications are commonly known as major tranquilizers. These medications are quite powerful and produce serious side effects. They must be used with great care, especially with third-age clients who are very sensitive to medications. It is essential to begin treatment with low dosages, and monitor carefully for desired effects (such as diminution of frequency and degree of psychotic symptoms like delusions and hallucinations) and for side effects. Caregivers and family members should be informed so they can watch for specific side effects and adverse reactions. Ongoing communication between the prescribing physician and caregivers regarding the observed effects of the medication is essential. Some of the commonly prescribed antipsychotic medications are:

Brand Name	Generic Name
CLOZARIL	clozapine
COMPAZINE	prochlorperazine
HALDOL	haloperidol
LOXITANE	loxapine
MELLARIL, MILLAZINE	thioridazine
MOBAN	molindone
NAVANE	thiothixene
PROLIXIN, PERMITIL	fluphenazine
SERENTIL	mesoridazine
STELAZINE, SUPRAZINE	trifluoperazine
THORAZINE	chlorpromazine
TRILAFON	perphenazine

Side Effects

Because all psychiatric medications possess the potential for serious side effects, clients and family should be informed about the possibility of this. Each individual is different. Given a specific medication, one person will experience side effects while another will not. If side effects do appear, they may decrease or disappear as the body adjusts to the medication. It is important that the initial dosage be low. Low dosages give the body a chance to adjust to the medication. If side effects do appear, their intensity will be lower at a low dosage. If serious side effects occur, or the medication does not produce the desired effects, either the dosage or the medication itself will likely have to be changed.

Continuous monitoring of the effects of medication is crucial. The client (if appropriate), the family and caregiver, the counselor, and the psychiatrist should all participate in the monitoring process. Communication among all involved can best safeguard the health of the client.

Appendix 9

Resources

The following books have contributed to the formation of my perspective on counseling third-age people:

Archer, James, Jr. *Managing Anxiety and Stress*. Muncie, IN: Accelerated Development, Inc., 1982.

Averty, Anne C., with Furst, Edith and Hummel, Donna, Ph.D. *Successful Aging: A Sourcebook for Older People and Their Families*. New York: Ballantine Books, 1987.

Beattie, Melody. *Beyond Codependency: And Getting Better All The Time*. New York: Harper/Hazelden, 1989.

Beavers, W. Robert, M.D., and Hampson, Robert, Ph.D. *Successful Families: Assessment and Intervention*. New York: W.W. Norton & Company, 1990.

Beck, Aaron T., Rush, A. John, Shaw, Brian F. and Emery, Gary. *Cognitive Therapy of Depression*. New York: The Guilford Press, 1979.

Belsky, Janet. *The Psychology of Aging: Theory, Research, and Practice*. Monterey, CA: Brooks/Cole Publishing Company, 1984.

Betland, Theodore. *Fitness for Life: Exercises for People Over 50*. Glenview, IL: Scott, Foresman and Company, 1986.

Black, Claudia, Ph.D., M.S.W. *"It Will Never Happen to Me": Children of Alcoholics*. New York: Ballantine Books, 1981.

Brink, T.L., Ph.D. *Clinical Gerontology: A Guide to Assessment and Intervention*. New York: The Haworth Press, 1986.

Brocklehurst, J.C., Tallis, R.C., and Fillit, H.M. *Textbook of Geriatric Medicine and Gerontology*. Edinburg, London, Madrid, Melbourne, New York, & Tokyo: Churchill Livingstone, 1992.

Brown, Robert, with Legal Counsel for the Elderly. *The Rights of Older Persons* (Second Edition). Carbondale/Edwardsville, IL: Southern Illinois University Press, 1989.

Burns, David D., M.D. *Feeling Good: The New Mood Therapy*. New York: New American Library, 1980.

Cailliet, Rene, M.D. and Gross, Leonard. *The Rejuvenation Strategy: A Medically Approved Fitness Program to Reverse the Effects of Aging*. Garden City, NY: Doubleday & Company, 1987.

Carkhuff, Robert R. *The Art of Helping VI*. Amhurst, MS: Human Resources Development Press, Inc., 1987.

Carstensen, Laura L,. and Edelstein, Barry A. *Handbook of Clinical Gerontology*. New York: Pergamon Press, 1987.

Cohen, Donna, Ph.D. and Eisdorfer, Carl, Ph.D., M.D. *The Loss of Self: A Family Resource for the Care of Alzheimer's Disease and Related Disorders*. New York: W.W. Norton & Company, 1986.

Cormjet, L. Sherilyn and Hackney, Harold. *The Professional Counselor: A Process Guide to Helping*. Englewood Cliffs, NJ: Prentice Hall, Inc.

Ellis, Albert, Ph.D. and Harper, Robert A., Ph.D. *A New Guide to Rational Living*. North Hollywood, CA: Wilshire Book Company, 1975.

Engler, Jack, Ph.D. and Goleman, Daniel, Ph.D. *The Consumer's Guide to Psychotherapy*. New York: Simon and Shuster, 1992.

Fry, P.S. Depression, *Stress, and Adaptation in the Elderly: Psychological Assessment and Intervention*. Rockbridge, MD: Aspen Publishers, Inc., 1986.

Gilhooly, Mary L.M., Zarit, Steven H., and Birren, James E., Editors. *The Dementias: Policy and Management*. Englewood Cliffs, NJ: Prentice-Hall, 1986.

Gorman, Jack M., M.D. *Essential Guide to Psychiatric Drugs.* New York: St. Martin's Press, 1990.

Heitler, Susan, Ph.D. *From Conflict to Resolution: Strategies for Diagnosis and Treatment of Distressed Individuals, Couples, and Families.* New York: W.W. Norton & Company, 1990.

Jotto, Anthony F. *A Guide to the Understanding of Alzheimer's Disease and Related Disorders.* Washington Square, NY: New York University Press, 1987.

Kagan, Richard and Schlosberg, Shirley. *Families in Perpetual Crisis.* New York: W.W. Norton & Company, 1989.

Mace, Nancy L. and Rabins, Peter V., M.D. *The 36-Hour Day: A Family Guide to Caring for Persons with Alzheimer's Disease, Related Dementing Disease, and Memory Loss in Later Life.* Baltimore: The Johns Hopkins University Press, 1981.

Masters, William H., Johnson, Virginia E., and Kolodny, Robert C. *Human Sexuality,* (Third Edition). Glenview, IL: Scott, Foresman and Company, 1988.

Nelson, Eugene C., D.Sc., Roberts, Ellen, M.P.H., Simmons, Jeannette, D. Sc., and Tilsdale, William A., M.D. *Medical and Health Guide for People Over Fifty.* Glenview, IL: Scott, Foresman and Company, 1986.

Patterson, C.H. *Theories of Counseling and Psychotherapy* (Fourth Edition). New York: Harper & Row, 1986.

Rogers, C.R. *Client-Centered Therapy: Its Current Practice, Implications, and Theory.* Boston: Houghton Mifflin, 1951.

Rubin, Lillian B. *Intimate Strangers: Men and Women Together.* New York: Harper & Row, 1983.

Salzman, Bernard, M.D. *Handbook of Psychiatric Drugs: A Consumer's Guide to Safe and Effective Use.* New York: Henry Holt & Co., 1991.

Sanford, Linda Tschirhart and Donovan, Mary Ellen. *Women and Self-Esteem: Understanding and Improving the Way We Think and Feel About Ourselves.* Garden City, NY: Anchor Press/Doubleday, 1984.

Sheehy, Gail. *Passages: Predictable Crises of Adult Life*. New York: Bantam Books, 1976.

Stoppard, Dr. Miriam. *The Best Years of Your Lives*. New York: Ballantine Books, 1983.

Worden, J. William, Ph.D. *Grief Counseling and Grief Therapy: A Handbook for the Mental Health Practitioner*. New York: Springer Publishing Company, 1982.

Tatelbaum, Judy. *The Courage to Grieve*. New York: Lippincott & Crowell, 1980.

Index